SHAKIN' THE KETCHUP BOT'LE

SHAKIN' THE KETCHUP BOT'LE

A fascinating collection of ideas, anecdotes, observations
and some really curious bits culled from
QUEST, the magazine of the
Queen's English Society –

with a Foreword by Gyles Brandreth

Edited by James Alexander
Advisory group: Sidney Callis, Michael Gorman
Cartoons © 2008 by Nathan Ariss

THE UNIVERSITY OF BUCKINGHAM PRESS

First published in Great Britain in 2008 by
The University of Buckingham Press
Buckingham MK18 1EG

A CIP catalogue record for this book is available at the British
Library

ISBN 10 0-9554642-7-7
ISBN 13 978-0-9554642-7-0

FOREWORD

Language is power. It is what defines us and differentiates us from the animals and those whose hands do trail upon the ground. As the philosopher said, 'No matter how eloquently a dog may bark, he cannot tell you that his parents were poor but honest.' Language does that.

Language is power and, happily, of all the many and varied languages of the world none is richer – or more potent – than the English language. Ours is a mongrel tongue that has grown and developed over a thousand years. To mix metaphors (and that's the joy of language: you can do with it what you will), it is a flowing river of words fed by an extraordinary assortment of tributaries.

India gave us 'bungalow'. Germany gave us 'blitz'. Shakespeare introduced 'leapfrog' to the language. Lewis Carroll conjured up 'chortle' and 'galumph'. The 1914-18 war threw up 'scrounge' and 'camouflage'. World War II led to 'wishful thinking'. Old words vanish (what a shame we don't call a 'hiccup' a 'yex' any more*), new words come along ('automation' made it into the dictionary in the year that I was born; 'incremental' is more recent). The story of the English language is full of change and decay and pleasant surprises. 'The big cheese' comes not from cheese, but from the Hindi *chiz*; 'blindworms' are neither blind nor worms: they are legless lizards that can see.

I love the English language. I love its richness, its range, its possibilities. I love the fun you can have with it. I love the arguments you can have about it! For all these reasons, and

* Did I mean to write 'hiccough'?

more, I love the Queen's English Society. The Society was founded in 1972 with an unambiguous mission: 'to promote the maintenance, knowledge, understanding, development and appreciation of the English language as used both colloquially and in literature; to educate the public in its correct and elegant usage; and to discourage the intrusion of anything detrimental to clarity or euphony.'

The Society celebrates our language and aims to protect the best of its traditions, defending unashamedly the precision, subtlety and richness of our parent tongue against 'debasement, ambiguity and other forms of misuse'. And through its journal, *Quest*, the Society provides a unique forum for intelligent debate about every aspect of written and spoken English.

If, like me, you are fascinated by words and love our language, you are in for a treat. You have in your hands a collection of some of the most entertaining, erudite, and stimulating material that *Quest* has published over the years. Enjoy!

Gyles Brandreth

2008

CONTENTS

Items preceded by a bullet (•) are, shall we say, the less serious items.

THE QUEEN'S ENGLISH SOCIETY

The objects of the Queen's English Society are to promote and uphold the use of good English, and to encourage the enjoyment of the language. The Society aims to defend the precision, subtlety and marvellous richness of our language against debasement, ambiguity and other forms of misuse.

The Society strongly advocates a return to the formal teaching of English in schools. It agrees with the testing of pupils and with the need for all teachers to correct their pupils' errors in a helpful way. Children must be brought up to recognise that there is a formal structure to the language, and that the literature of the past is a worthy and useful source of writing style. Although it accepts that there is always a natural development of any language, the Society deplores those changes which are the result of ignorance, and which become established because of indifference.

There have been enough media reports to convince all of us that young people now leave school with a quite meagre understanding of grammar, punctuation and spelling: one might even say that many are completely unaware of the existence of any formal rules. These reports are certainly substantiated by surveys conducted by the Society.

The Society hopes to attract those who are interested in, and knowledgeable about, the English language. It is not necessary to be academically expert: it is your keenness to help us in our fight against the palpable decay of English that matters most.

QUEST

The Society's journal, *Quest*, is published quarterly. The Editor welcomes original articles, material from other sources, and letters. The items appearing in this book are all taken from *Quest* and, for the most part, are presented in chronological order. This means that some of the ideas discussed in earlier items might be re-examined in later pieces, and readers will very likely be intrigued that topics that were of tremendous interest and concern in the 1980s and 1990s may nowadays seem less (or more) important and relevant – such is the fluidity of language and the presence of ever-on-going discussions and confrontations amongst speakers, writers, linguists, academics and Johnny foreigner!

Authorship – many articles in the magazine are published anonymously or over simple initials. Where we can positively attribute authorship, we have done so in this book. To folk who recognise their unattributed piece, we apologise, and hope that they will continue to write for us. The QES advisory group and the editor are hugely grateful for all the contributions to the magazine over the years and especially to those writers, acknowledged or not, who have had pieces chosen for this unique anthology.

GUESS WHO WROTE THIS

The following was written in 1930, nearly 80 years ago. Can you identify the author?

'In a sensible language like English important words are connected and related to one another by other little words. The Romans in that stern antiquity considered such a method weak and unworthy. Nothing would satisfy them but that the structure of every word should be reacted on by its neighbours in accordance with elaborate rules to meet the different conditions in which it might be used. There is no doubt that this method both sounds and looks more impressive than our own. The sentence fits together like a piece of polished machinery. Every phrase can be tensely charged with meaning. It must have been very laborious, even if you were brought up to it: but no doubt it gave the Romans, and the Greeks too, a fine and easy way of establishing their posthumous fame. They were the first-comers in the fields of thought and literature. When they arrived at fairly obvious reflections upon life and love, upon war, fate or manners, they coined them into slogans or epigrams for which their language was so well adapted, and thus preserved the patent rights for all time. Hence their reputation. Nobody ever told me this at school. I have thought it all out in later life.

'But even as a schoolboy I questioned the aptness of the Classics for the prime structure of our education. So they told me how Mr Gladstone read Homer for fun, which I thought served him right; and that it would be a great pleasure to me in after life. When I seemed incredulous, they added that Classics would be a help in writing or speaking English. They then pointed out the number of our modern words which are derived from the Latin or Greek. Apparently one could use these words much better, if one knew the exact source from which they had sprung. I was fain to admit a practical value. But now even this has been swept away. The foreigners and the Scots have joined together to introduce a pronunciation of Latin which divorces it finally from the English tongue. They tell us to pronounce audience 'owdience'; and civil 'keywheel'. They have distorted one of my most serviceable and impressive quotations into the ridiculous booby 'Wainy, Weedy, Weeky'. Punishment should be reserved for those who have spread this evil.'

(Not sure who this was? Check the answer on page 177)

SOME CURIOUS DEFINITIONS

Authoritative works of reference are invaluable but, here are some irreverent definitions given by Ambrose Bierce in his *Devil's Dictionary*.

DICTIONARY   A malevolent literary device for cramping the growth of a language and making it hard and inelastic.

EDUCATION   That which discloses to the wise and disguises from the foolish their lack of understanding.

GRAMMAR   A system of pitfalls thoughtfully prepared for the feet of the self-made man, along the path by which he advances to distinction.

LEARNING   The kind of ignorance distinguishing the studious.

LEXICOGRAPHER   A pestilent fellow who, under the pretence of recording some particular stage in the development of a language, does what he can to arrest its growth, stiffen its flexibility and mechanise its methods. For your lexicographer, having written his dictionary, comes to be considered as one having authority, whereas his function is only to make a record, not to give a law. The natural servility of the human understanding having invested him with judicial power, surrenders its right of reason and submits itself to a chronicle as if it were a statute.

QUOTATION   The act of repeating erroneously the words of another.

JARGON CORNER

The word 'jargon' is used in various ways. Sir Ernest Gowers, in *The Complete Plain Words*, applied it to technical terms and conventional phrases which were understood by the initiated, but which were unintelligible to outsiders.

The use of a characteristic language, technical, legal, or otherwise, which aids communication between members of a trade or profession, is perfectly respectable and is probably necessary for concise thought and expression, although the definition in the Shorter Oxford English Dictionary implies that it is usually used contemptuously.

In one of his Cambridge Lectures, Sir Arthur Quiller-Couch had this to say on jargon:

'If your language be Jargon, your intellect, if not your whole character, will almost certainly correspond. Where your mind should go straight, it will dodge: the difficulties it should approach with a fair front and grip with a firm hand it will be seeking to evade or circumvent. For the Style is the Man, and where a man's treasure is there his heart and his brain, and his writing, will be also.'

It seems that Sir Arthur Quiller-Couch regarded jargon as being related to its archaic meaning of the twittering of birds and its use could only cloud thought and understanding.

In *The Jargon of the Professions*, Kenneth Hudson suggests that jargon should contain four essential elements.

1. It reflects a particular profession or occupation.

2. It is pretentious, with only a small kernel of meaning within it.

3. It is used mainly by intellectually inferior people, who feel a need to convince the general public of their importance.

4. It is, deliberately or accidentally, mystifying.

The following example seems to meet all the criteria of Sir Arthur Quiller-Couch and Mr Hudson:

'The symptom pattern previously delineated as the stress response

in a mental health setting was hypothesised to be useful in conceptualising reactions to a traumatic event in a nonpsychiatric population.'

Yes, that was written in all seriousness by a supposedly educated person, a physician, in the *Journal of the American Medical Association* (5th October, 1979, page 1499), and the editor let it be printed. Even allowing for the peculiarities of medical communication, this is the worst piece of jargon that I have met for many years, the veritable nadir of medical writing.

I assume it means that the symptoms due to stress in normal people are similar to those in psychiatric patients in similar circumstances and, therefore, experience with those who are mentally ill can be used to predict responses in those who are not.

BBC PRONUNCIATION

Graham Pointon – Pronunciation Advisor to the BBC

The BBC has long worried about the standards of pronunciation, and usage, broadcast on its airwaves. This concern resulted first in the Advisory Committee on Spoken English, formed in 1926 with Robert Bridges as Chairman. This committee had as its main task not to decide which pronunciation of contentious words was the correct one, as many people believed, but to recommend one pronunciation which all announcers and newsreaders should adopt when on the air. So, although it recommended 'controversy', with stress on the first syllable, it did not thereby decide that 'controversy', with second syllable stress, was wrong. The recommendations were based on the usage of 'educated' people – whatever that word might mean. On the death of Robert Bridges, George Bernard Shaw became Chairman, and he remained as Chairman until the late thirties. Among the members of the Committee were two very distinguished phoneticians, Daniel Jones, Professor of Phonetics at University College, London, who remained closely associated with the BBC until his death in 1967, and Arthur Lloyd James, Lecturer, later Professor of Phonetics, at the School of Oriental and African Studies, who was the Committee's Honorary Secretary.

Having first issued a booklet, *Broadcast English I: recommendations to announcers regarding certain words of doubtful pronunciation*, which went into three editions, each one larger than the last, the Committee turned its attention to proper names and published six further booklets, *Broadcast English II – VII*, dealing successively with English, Scottish, Welsh, Northern Irish and foreign place-names, and British family names and titles. An eighth booklet was prepared and printed, dealing with the pronunciation of some foreign personal names, but I am not certain that it was published officially. By now it was 1939 and the Second World War had broken out. There were more important tasks for committees of eminent people than establishing pronunciations to be used by the BBC and no more meetings were called. The BBC did not consider the task useless, however, and Professor Lloyd James's secretary, Miss Gertrude (pronounced Elizabeth) M. Miller became the BBC's first Pronunciation Assistant. Initially the Pronunciation Unit had a staff of three, two linguists and a typist. This grew to five temporarily but it is now reduced to four. Miss Miller retired in 1971, to be succeeded by Mrs Hazel Wright, and I became the third Head of the Unit in January 1979.

Sometimes we are flattered by members of the public who credit us with enormous power to dictate the manner in which all the Corporation's employees should pronounce all words from 'and', or 'but', to 'ululation' and beyond. However, we neither have this power, nor do we seek to gain it. Our role is mainly advisory and mainly concerned with proper names.

With such a small staff, it is clear that we cannot assess all scripts for pronunciation before they are broadcast, nor can we monitor all broadcasts for mistakes. For the most part, we are reliant on broadcasters coming to us for advice and this keeps us all very busy.

Our day begins at 9 am and continues until 6 pm, Monday to Friday. During those hours there is always someone in the office to answer the telephone or personal enquiries. We maintain a card index, mainly of people and places, but also including technical terms, a category we call 'Music and Literature' (titles of works, characters from books and plays, names of musical instruments, etc.), names of aircraft and ships, and miscellaneous – phrases or words in foreign languages which have been used in programmes. We have quite a collection of 'Happy Birthday', 'Merry Christmas' and 'Happy New Year' in different languages!

The index is available throughout the 24 hours and we have daughter indexes at relevant places in the BBC – newsrooms and continuity suites, although these do not contain as much background information as the master index.

Each morning one of us compiles a news list of names we think likely to be appearing in bulletins during the day. This is based on the morning's newspapers and news prospects put out by the newsroom. Other names are added as they arise during the day. The list is sent to all news output points in the BBC, with our recommendations in a modified spelling, twice a day by telex (at noon and at 4 pm) and also in more permanent form on a printed sheet. Many of the names are already in our index, which, in the course of 40 years, has grown to about 100,000 items, but it is rare for a day to pass by without a new name appearing for this list. We then have to do some research and, clearly, with an estimated 4,000 languages in the world, we cannot know how to pronounce them all. Our primary resource for foreign names is the External Services of the BBC. The BBC broadcasts in 39 languages and the various sections at Bush House have native speakers of many more than that number. If we cannot find a native speaker at Bush House, then there are Embassies, Trade Centres, Tourist Offices, all usually willing to help us pronounce their language correctly. For names in Britain, which can be as difficult as any with its Ruthvens (pronounced <u>rivv</u>en) and Milngavies (pronounced mul<u>gi</u>), we try to contact either the individual concerned, or a close friend or relative, or, in the case of place names, the local vicar or Post Office. Welsh and Gaelic names we get from the BBC in Cardiff and Glasgow, always from a native speaker of the language concerned.

We play no part in the selection process for people who are to broadcast and I cannot comment on the accents, or other qualities, of newsreaders, announcers, journalists, or others. At one time it was thought that all newsreaders and announcers should speak Received Pronunciation, which implied a certain type of education and was supposed to guarantee a degree of authority in such a speaker's voice. It is now accepted that one need not be a Received Pronunciation speaker in order to be authoritative and well-educated, nor for one to speak clearly, and accents more closely associated with a particular area of the country are now to be heard. It is well to remember that, although Received Pronunciation is not confined to a definite area within England, it is nevertheless a regional accent: its speakers are all English, not Scottish, Welsh, Irish, American, or Antipodean. Any Scot, like Lord Home, who speaks Received Pronunciation, is considered by other Scots to have an English accent.

There is nothing certain in the language except that it is in a constant state of flux. The BBC must reflect this situation but we do not believe we should lead. 'Dispute' as a noun may be heard from outside contributors; it is not a neologism but the standard pronunciation in the North of England. Until it is well established throughout British English, if this ever happens, we shall continue to recommend 'dispute' for both noun and verb.

Editorial note *This piece was written some twenty years ago. It is entertaining to note how much more often the incidence of regional accents and differently pronounced words can be found these days, within the BBC, and indeed even more so with other broadcasters.*

✳ ✳ ✳ *BREAK ...*

The chippie and the Polish pilots

One pun that delighted us when we heard it for the first time some years ago concerned the person in the monastery who was responsible for cooking the fish and chips on Fridays – the chip monk, sometimes known as the fish friar!

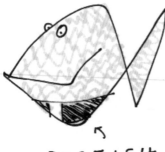

DOGFISH
COLLAR

Three Polish fighter pilots were attending a party given by an English hostess during World War II. She asked one of them if he had any children. 'No,' he replied, 'my wife is inconceivable.' Upon which the second pilot intervened to explain: 'No, he means his wife is unbearable.' The third pilot shook his head. 'You must pardon their English. What they mean to say is that his wife is impregnable.'

DO WE NEED AN ENGLISH ACADEMY ALONG THE LINES OF THE ACADÉMIE FRANCAISE?

Who is the arbiter of English grammar, style, usage and pronunciation? The French have their Académie, but we do not appear to have anything similar.

As everyone knows, and many may have pondered the reason, England (unlike France and Italy) has no authoritative linguistic academy to give clear rulings on questions of language. According to a leading authority, Dr Simeon Potter, linguistic societies do exist: they include the British Academy, the Philological Society, the English Association and the Committee on Spoken English of the BBC, but none has laid claim to any kind of authority or supervisory powers.

The British Academy claims to promote the study of the moral and political sciences, including history, philosophy, law, political economy, archaeology and philology. Its Fellows have included eminent philologists like Dr Henry Bradley and Sir William Craigie. The Philological Society, re-organised in 1842, met with the object of investigating the structure, affinities and history of language. They compiled an important dictionary of hitherto unpublished texts in Old and Middle English, which is universally recognised to be the highest authority on the use of the English languages. The English Association, founded in 1906, is a society of unrestricted membership which seeks by means of lectures, readings, discussions, conferences and publications to unite and introduce to one another those who are interested in the English language and literature, whether as writers, teachers, artists, actors or administrators, and to uphold the standard of English writing and speech. In the early days of broadcasting, the BBC Advisory Committee on Spoken English was constituted to help those whose daily duty it was to broadcast the world's news, beginning its work in 1926. No special authority is claimed for the pronunciations recommended.

During 1913-1947 the Society for Pure English founded by Robert Bridges exercised its salutary influence with a series of informative tracts. Bridges believed that much could be done to preserve the purity of English in the fullest and best sense, not by foolish interference with living developments, but by agreeing upon a modest and practical scheme for informing popular taste on sound principles, for guiding educational authorities, and for introducing into practice certain slight modifications and advantageous changes. The Society eventually perished from dearth of scholarship, and material of the quality originally envisaged by the Founders.

According to Dr Potter, who was writing in 1950, linguistic societies are reluctant to assume responsibility for the control of good usage because few people regard such control as desirable or practicable. Both attempts to found a linguistic academy in England have failed.

The first in 1664 is associated with Dryden through the infant Royal Society which showed an active interest in language as an instrument of scientific thought, and set up a committee to improve the English language. This consisted of twenty-two people including John Dryden and John Evelyn among its members. Lacking drive and energy, it achieved little, so that as the Royal Society increased in strength, the attention of its Fellows became more absorbed by scientific research.

The second attempt made in 1712 is associated with Swift, who sent to the Earl of Oxford, Lord Treasurer, *A Proposal for Correcting, Improving and Ascertaining* (i.e. making certain) *the English Tongue*. It was well received. However Queen Anne died in 1714 and the Earl of Oxford together with his fellow Tories lost power. The ideas embodied in the *Proposal* were therefore never implemented, mainly for political reasons.

Swift, Addison, Pope and others who were active during the Age of Reason had often discussed the production of a Standard English Dictionary. This need was met by Samuel Johnson in 1755. Other grammars followed. As the century wore on, scepticism increased as to the desirability of embalming the language by the formation of an Academy. Johnson, whose influence was paramount, had flirted with the idea, but eventually felt that the loss would outweigh the gain. By the end of the 18th century, correctness of language was felt to be a relative term, not to be prescribed by any sort of Committee: it was to be measured by the standards of good use or the best use of the best writers.

A number of important grammars appeared culminating in *A New English Grammar – Logical and Historical* which was published in two volumes in 1892 and 1898 by the greatest of all English philologists, Henry Sweet. Language, wrote Sweet, is partly rational, partly irrational and arbitrary. Apart from Sweet's work, no comprehensive English grammars have been produced in

English. By far the most elaborate English grammars have been compiled by three Dutchmen, H Poutsma, Etsko Kruisinga and RW Zandvoort, and by the Dane, Otto Jespersen. The last produced the first part of his *Modern English Grammar on Historical Principles* in 1909. The work was completed in 1949 by three of his former pupils in the University of Copenhagen. Primarily a description of living English with an historical outlook, Jespersen professed to represent English grammar not as a set of stiff dogmatic precepts according to which some things are correct and others absolutely wrong, but as something living and developing under continual fluctuations and undulations, something that is founded on the past and prepares the way for the future, something that is not always consistent or perfect, but progressing and perfectible – in one word, human. Although widely honoured by scholars the world over, Jespersen disclaimed any right to tell British and American readers what is correct or pure English, but only to register and, if possible, to explain the actual facts of English usage in various periods.

Jespersen, according to Dr Potter, believed in progress in language and regarded English as a language in a very advanced stage. But what is progress in language, asks Dr Potter. Jespersen's *New English Dictionary on Historical Principles*, now generally called the *Oxford English Dictionary*, appeared in instalments from 1883 – 1928. Its first editor, Sir James Murray was responsible for nearly half the entire work. He was later assisted by Henry Bradley, Sir William Craigie and Charles Talbut Onions. It aims at exhibiting the history and signification of words now in use or known to have been in use since the middle of the 12th century. No other language in the world possesses such a complete guide on all aspects of our language. On matters of pronunciation, Professor Daniel Jones' *An English Pronouncing Dictionary*, 1948, professes to record the sounds of typical Southern English people in ordinary conversation. It is a record of a form of speech which, says Dr Potter, is both intelligible and pleasing to the greatest number of educated people throughout the English-speaking world.

ON SPELLING – DOES IT MATTER ?

One of the questions most frequently asked by children in a new class is: 'Please, Miss, does the spelling matter?' Presumably the questioner could spell correctly if necessary, but otherwise it would be too much trouble.

My usual answer to this query was to write on the blackboard a sentence from the work of a first-year boy: 'John Gilpin rowed a horse.' This invariably caused much merriment as the bright ones took the point at once.

I found that it was necessary to teach grammar in the French and German classes, though it seems nowadays that it is considered unnecessary to bother with grammar in English lessons.

One day the English Inspector came into my room halfway through an English lesson. He listened until the end, then after I had dismissed the class he said accusingly: 'You were teaching them grammar.' When I assured him that they had a grammar lesson every Wednesday, he protested that grammar was unnecessary and that I was inhibiting their ideas. I could not help retorting that Milton and Shakespeare did not seem to have been inhibited by receiving a thorough grounding in grammar.

Some time later the point was discussed at a staff meeting in which the Deputy Head declared that teaching grammar was totally unnecessary. 'After all,' he said, 'we all speak quite naturally and correctly without stopping to think about verbs and nouns.'

'Do we?' I thought, but aloud I merely suggested that if grammatical speech had become a habit with us, it was probably because we had all learned it so thoroughly at school.

 **BREAK ...**

English is a crazy language

Let's face it – English is a crazy language. There is no egg in eggplant nor ham in hamburger; neither apple nor pine in pineapple. English muffins weren't invented in England or French fries in France. Sweetmeats are candies while sweetbreads, which aren't sweet, are meat.

We take English for granted. But if we explore its paradoxes, we find that quicksand can work slowly, boxing rings are square and a guinea pig is neither from Guinea nor is it a pig.

And why is it that writers write but fingers don't fing, grocers don't groce and hammers don't ham? If the plural of tooth is teeth, why isn't the plural of booth beeth? One goose, two geese. So one loose tooth, two leese teeth? One index, two indices?

Doesn't it seem crazy that you can make amends but not an amend, that you comb through annals of history but not a single annal? If you have a bunch of odds and ends and get rid of all but one of them, what do you call it?

If teachers have taught, why haven't preachers praught? If a vegetarian eats vegetables, what does a humanitarian eat? If you wrote a letter, perhaps you bote your tongue? Sometimes I think all the English speakers should be committed to an asylum for the verbally insane. In what language do people recite at a play and play at a recital? Ship by truck and send cargo or a truck by ship? Have noses that run and feet that smell? Park on driveways and drive on parkways? Lift a thumb to thumb a lift? Table a plan in order to plan a table?

How can a slim chance and a fat chance be the same, while a wise man and wise guy are opposites? How can overlook and oversee be opposites, while quite a lot and quite a few are alike? How can a person be 'pretty ugly'?

How can the weather be hot as hell one day and cold as hell another. Have you noticed that we talk about certain things only when they are absent? Have you ever seen a horseful carriage or a strapful gown? Met a sung hero or experienced requited love? Have you ever run into someone who was combobulated, gruntled, ruly or peccable? And where are all those people who really are spring chickens or who would actually hurt a fly?

You have to marvel at the unique lunacy of a language in which your house can burn up as it burns down, in which you fill in a form by filling it out and in which an alarm clock goes off by going on. Why is 'crazy man' an insult, while to insert a comma and say 'crazy, man!' is a compliment (as when applauding a jazz performance).

English was invented by people, not computers, and it reflects the creativity of the human race (which, of course, isn't a race at all). That is why, when the stars are out, they are visible, but when the lights are out, they are invisible. And why, when I wind up my watch, I start it, but when I wind up this piece, I end it.

THE LANGUAGE of THE ALTERNATIVE SERVICE BOOK

The Rev Peter Nourse, MA

From the literary point of view, the language of the Church's *Alternative Service Book* obviously bears no comparison with that of the *Book of Common Prayer* which possesses the very highest literary quality. A factor which probably accounts for this rare literary quality is the survival of what is technically known as the cursus, i.e. the flow of cadence in English prose, derived originally from Latin prose, the beauty of which depended on the arrangement of long and short syllables, specially at the end of a sentence. The early compilers of liturgical prayers made use, with some modifications, of the rules of Cicero – particularly the cursus. Although it may seem to be be extraordinary that a system which suited Latin prose could be utilised successfully in English prose, there are nevertheless innumerable examples to be found in the first English Prayer Book of 1549; these are mostly to be found in the clause-endings of the Collects, in the ending of the Psalms, and in the Litany. It is not really surprising that Cranmer and his associates, in their translation from the Latin, should have tried to retain the same rhythmic flow in English. It is this, of course, which makes the language of the *Book of Common Prayer* so outstanding in literary quality.

The attempt to modernise the language of worship in the *Alternative Service Book* can only be regarded as literary Philistinism, for which even the improvements in liturgical arrangement do not compensate. If the shape of the liturgy had been thus improved whilst the incomparable English of the 1662 Prayer Book were retained, apart from the possible alteration of a very few words of which the meaning has changed, the *Alternative Service Book* might have been a volume of enduring literary merit. It is very much to be regretted that a quite creditable liturgical revision has been ruined by such a lamentable attempt to improve the language of the *Book of Common Prayer* – an attempt which has failed dismally.

ARCTIC, RECOGNISE and CONTRIBUTE – ON INTERESTING WORDS

SS Eustace

Consider the pronunciation 'artic' for 'arctic'. The word has an interesting history. It comes from the Medieval French 'artique', whose pronunciation is well enough shown by Chaucer's 'artik' 1391, the first occurrence in English. The Oxford Dictionary does not record 'arctic' till 1549. 'Arctic' shows well the effect of the Renaissance, the rebirth of classical learning: someone thought to alter the spelling as if the word had been taken from the Latin 'arcticus', and the pronunciation was gradually accommodated to this error in the latter 18th century. Thus in 1757 a pronouncing dictionary spells it 'artick', implying 'artik' as the only pronunciation; in 1764 another one says it is spelt 'arctic' but sounded 'artik'; not till 1773 does a pronouncing dictionary give both the spelling 'arctic' and the sound 'arktik'.

So it is not a little interesting that 'artik', or rather 'ahtik', is still current to-day. Incidentally the popular 'reconise' has a similar history: French 'reconnuiss-' 1456, Latinised to 'recognise' 1531 – also compare 'recognition' 1473.

There are also two pronunciations of 'contribute', English since 1530:

1. 'contr*i*bute' – influenced by Latin 'contr*i*buo' (present tense). This stressing is known from scansion in Skelton 1460 – 1529 (?), in 1731 etc. (Bailey's dictionary), 1788 (Cowper) and generally, even in dictionaries by the Novocastrian Spence 1775 and the Yorkshireman Enfield 1809 – at least I guess he was a Yorkshireman, because of the dialect words – and

2. 'c*o*ntribute', influenced by Latin 'c*o*ntrib*u*tus' (past participle) and by 'c*o*ntrib*u*tion', English since 1387. The stressing 'c*o*ntribute' is given in 1570 (Levins, *Manipulus Vocabulorum*) and is known from scansion in 1592 (Marlowe), 1635 (May) and 1667 (Milton); in 1704 it is suggested by alliteration and rhythm in prose (Addison); 1855 (Worcester's dictionary, 'some persons, erroneously') and 1893 (Oxford dictionary, 'formerly dialectal'). Which dialect? We associate it with the North Country, where old variants often survive. Levins was Yorkshire but Marlowe was from Kent and May probably from Sussex, while Milton was a Londoner. Poetic licence does not embrace the outlandish.

ON THE SHADY SIDE

SR O'Hanlon

It is an inescapable fact that there has been some etymological confidence trick in our acceptance of the word *umbrella* to identify a form of portable canopy to protect the person against the more inclement elements of rain, sleet and snow, or any admixture thereof. Conceived out of the Latin *ombra* and followed by an Italianate accouchement, the word properly and specifically relates to shade – an ambient condition seldom needed to be sought in the outer islands of the European Common Market. The French and Germans have done rather better with respectively their *parapluie* and *Regenschirm*.

Had Mr Jonas Hanway been content to merchandise his woollen goods in his native land instead of frequenting the bazaars of the Middle East, the appearance of umbrellas in the streets of eighteenth century London and the adoption of the inappropriate word might have been delayed long enough for an inspired neologism.

That there was nothing novel about the umbrella is well testified by the sculptured remains of ancient Egypt and the patterns on disinterred Greek vases, where it is revealed as a symbol of high rank. In India, too, resplendent princes claimed the title of Lords of the Umbrella, and in Burma white umbrellas were sacred to its kings and white elephants. All these, of course, were rightly providing shade. Much later and back home, the profane overtook the sacred when, with pin-striped suit and bowler hat, the umbrella became the symbol of the business man searching not so much for shade as for self-satisfaction and in no wise to be confused with the emblem of tribal chiefs which was designed to put their neighbours, rather than themselves, in the shade.

The ladies also, of course, subscribe to this form of pluvial insurance, but making up by colourful gaiety what their apparatus lacks in form construction. As for shade, however, umbrellas are never taken out on sunny days except by those unbelievers in meteorological forecasts or those dedicated to protest marches: which raises the question, whatever happened to the sunshade (Latin, *umbella*) or parasol (a splendid self-explanatory word of impeccable parentage) which, it is not too much to claim, was the hallmark of an age of elegance regrettably long departed?

I imagine there is now little hope of correcting the umbriferous misnomer. The Dickensian gamp, although still current in the colloquial byways of our language, hardly qualifies, and (my own small offering) weather-shield, although fulfilling the etymological requirements, has overtones of double glazing. So maybe we shall have to fall back on *brolly*. At least it disguises the shady associations to which I have taken such umbrage.

 **BREAK ...**

WHAT'S IN A NAME? GE Perrett

I don't think it likely that Somerset Maugham
Has ever attempted to infaugham
His readers that the Duke of Gloucester
Was once no more than a wicked impoucester,
Nor yet that at one time the Earl of Leicester
Performed as Good Queen Bess's jeicester
During one of her visits to the Vale of Belvoir,
By playing the part of Bottom the Welvoir.

But I think it more likely that someone named
    Beauchamp
Would always be ready and willing to teauchamp
That if they caught sight of a name spelt Chalmondeley
There was no need at all just to stare at it dalmondeley,
Nor on seeing a name that is written as Vaughan
Does one need to feel just a little faulaughan;

While someone who's known by the name of MacLeod
Must surely feel extremely preod
That a famous compatriot, one Douglas-Home,
Was once our Prime Minister, though he might fome
At the strange way the Somerset people say 'Frome'.

But of one thing I'm certain – if I were Lord Beaulieu,
I'd ensure all my letters concluded 'Yours treaulieu'.

AS SHE IS SPOKE – Does accent matter?

An Englishman who emigrated to the USA eight years ago has recently lodged a Civil Rights discrimination suit in Michigan, alleging that he was sacked from his job on a telephone answering bank, because he speaks English with an English accent. His employers thought it might be too difficult for Mid-Westerners to understand. He was, it seems, especially offended since he has received much hospitality from Americans because he is English. My accent has always been an 'opener' in being able to communicate with people, he said.

The writer received greater courtesy. She found it necessary to protest to the Pennsylvania Railroad Company, because an official had taken both her outward and return ticket to Washington. After telling her story to four separate clerks in the ticket hall, she asked why she had to tell the story so many times without any result? Back came the disarming reply that they had so enjoyed hearing English properly spoken they did not want her to stop. Don't ever lose your cute little accent, they said, like your ticket.

CLASS DISMISS!

How far is class responsible for standards of pronunciation? Why is it that so many people talk common when our common aim should be to recognise a common tongue – good standard English – Received Pronunciation – call it what you will. This is a vexed question which should in no way be confused with ideas on dialect, regional timbre, or even those perennial arguments about the syllable-accentuation of certain words.

How far should children's speech be corrected? And should foreigners endeavouring to understand our language be puzzled beyond words because the English they hear all around them is not Accepted or Received Pronunciation?

In a recent article (Divided by a Common Tongue) the question is answered by Helen Bryant who has recently returned to England after fifty years spent in the United States. She reminds us of Professor Higgins' question in *My Fair Lady* – 'Why can't the English teach their children how to speak?'

She concludes: 'Adherence to a working class mode of speech is certainly not forced on those below by those above. It seems rather to be deliberately retained by the workers as part of their armament in an Us-against-Them struggle. Could not both sides approach the problem amicably? On the one side, could that slightly arrogant timbre be dropped: on the other, could decent pronunciation be more vigorously, perhaps more ingeniously inculcated? I ask for no miracles, only that England cease to be two nations, speaking two tongues, and that a thousand-year struggle come to an end.'

✳ ✳ ✳ *BREAK ...*

ALBERTA WEATHER

How an Edmonton (Canada) newspaper explains the Weather – 'Alberta Synopsis'

The tale is told again. An ornery unstable airiness that has been loitering over Alberta for the last couple of days still refuses to budge and high-tail it out of the province.

The problem is that the air has hitched itself to a vertical low over Fort St John way and this hitching post is so sturdy that only time is going to loosen the knot.

This cantankerous critter, the upper low keeps on bringing his ugly buddies, the clouds and showers gang, into our peaceful regions and they stir up heaps of trouble before riding off into the horizon.

But yonder down south cowpokes will only gander at a few puffy white dogies skipping like tumbleweeds across the sky.

A POINT OF VIEW from THE HAGUE

James Brockway

I am of the conviction, difficult to prove, that many of the new, modish expressions absorbed into English during the past few years are, in fact, mistranslations from other languages, especially from German and Dutch. I also believe that most of the English who use these expressions – as though they were embellishments of our language and the chic and up-to-date thing to say – are unaware that they are merely parroting the mistakes made by translators, and by many foreigners when speaking our language.

Obviously, there is something ridiculous in such a situation. 'If only you knew...', one might say when listening to such speakers, several of them British politicians, journalists or broadcasters, all unwittingly engaged in spreading mistakes instead of enlightenment.

The recent rapid growth in the number of these expressions (I am thinking of such things as: that is something different again, to put at risk, every last man, and at this point in time) suggests that they originate in international organisations like the EEC and the UN, where nowadays translation (including mistranslation) proceeds apace, and where more and more persons whose mother tongue is not English are called upon to express themselves in our language.

I suspect, however, that another main – perhaps the chief – source is the United States, where English is the medium but where large sections of the population are of other than English origin, many having come from Germany, Holland and other European countries. These Americans – obliged like other foreign speakers at the EEC and the UN to use English – often translate literally from their mother tongue. The resulting expressions are all too readily adopted by us without our realising what we are doing; so that gradually, or not so gradually, the perfectly good English which should have been used is pushed out of our language and replaced by their inaccurate mistranslations. A simple example is a *high* (from the German *Höhe* or the Dutch *Hoogte*) for what we in English would call a peak. (An all-time high in unemployment). The examples are myriad, but here, in this brief space, I will confine myself to the first four mentioned.

That is something different again. This is a literal mistranslation of a German and Dutch expression which employs the redundant again when what is meant is simply that something is different. The Dutch always say for this: *Dat is weer vat anders* – literally 'That is again something different', when all they mean is: 'That's different.' Why should we adopt their long-windedness when 'That's different' will do? And if we want to refer to another thing that is different, why not simply 'That's different too,' rather than the clumsy Teutonic 'That is something different again'?

To put at risk. This, heard ad nauseam nowadays, stems from the German phrase *auf Spiel setzen*, a term derived from games of chance. The English verbs now being ousted from our language by this mistranslation are: to endanger, to imperil, to threaten or to jeopardise, as the case may be.

Every last man. It was some time before it occurred to me that this is of German and Dutch origin. The expression, originating in the United States where it is current and normal usage, is, of course, nonsensical, for there can be only one last man. At first, I imagined the mistake had come from a mishearing of our expression the very last man, before realising that it was yet another mistranslation. In German and Dutch, *alle* can mean both all and every; the Dutch for the very last man is *de aller laatste man*, and the German *der aller letzte Mann*, both of which expressions have been mistranslated as 'every last man' owing to a confusion of *alle* with *aller*.

At this point in time. This wordy ouster of our concise expressions 'now' or 'at the moment' is a mistranslation of the German *auf diesem Zeitpunkt* and the Dutch *op dit tijdstip* (at this time-point). It is of a pomposity and wordiness good English has always sought to avoid.

I said the examples are now myriad ... and they are! Here are just a few more, for each of which the literal German or Dutch equivalents can be traced: to stop off (to break the journey); to want out (to wish to get away); ten over two (ten past two); how come? (how is it that...?); a whole new flavour (an entirely new flavour – due to the German and Dutch adjective for whole being identical with the adverb for wholly); guidelines (guiding principles); path-breaking (pioneering); to bring you to the station (to take you to the station); to win (to produce – from the soil or a mine); hopefully (I/we hope etc.). There are countless others – new ones, it seems, being added every week.

Of course languages (especially ours which is in use world-wide) are always changing, always open to outside influences. Such change lies in their very nature; only a King Canute would seek to halt it. Many expressions adopted from foreign languages (American included!) are apt, handy and amusing – welcome imports which enliven the language, if not overdone. It is absurd, too, to attempt to lay down the law by declaring that you must say this; that you must never say that! For it is certain that people will say what they like, anyway. There are no laws more inept than those which people flout and which cannot, in any case, be enforced.

Nor, of course, would I suggest that any blame attaches to foreigners who mistranslate into our language. Would that we made as brave an effort to speak theirs!

No, I am merely concerned to point out that many new expressions are almost certainly mistranslations coming to us from a world that is now a Babel a-buzz with translation, and to express the view that we might do well to think twice before using them. At the moment too many of us adopt these mistakes most eagerly, without giving a moment's thought to their demerits, to the existence of better, simpler expressions, and to the absurdity of what we are doing – copying foreigners' mistakes when using our own tongue.

SHAKESPEARE HAD A WORD FOR IT

How many people are aware of the large number of words and phrases in use today which were also used by Shakespeare? Unhappily, the language of the great bard, like Latin, has been largely dismissed by many of the progressive teachers of today as old-fashioned and irrelevant.

Among the more everyday words are to 'budge', 'jogging', 'hoodwink', to 'harp', 'hard-luck', 'laughing-stock', 'topsy-turvey', 'tongue-tied', a 'double-dealer', 'helter-skelter', to 'be in stitches' (of laughter), to 'lie low', 'so-so', 'pickle', to 'hob-nob, 'foul play' and 'boggle'.

Expressions include the following: 'thereby hangs a tale', 'the more fool you', 'to kill with kindness', 'to sell...for a song', 'flesh and blood', 'everything is at six and seven', 'a leopard cannot change his spots', 'I could brain him', 'I'll send him packing', 'that would set my teeth on edge', 'to be eaten out of house and home', 'to be fubbed off', 'to rule the roost', 'to stir with the lark', 'pell-mell'.

Nowadays many such down-to-earth expressions as the above have been overtaken in the vocabulary of the young by downright obscenities – sad to say, the common people get commoner every day.

A THRILLING SHOCK

In an issue of *The Magistrate (*Vol.39 No.7), His Honour Judge Peter Mason QC refers to the language of the witness box as a thrilling shock after the pretentious gobbledygook of social enquiry reports.

Ordinary men tell their stories in their own particular way: 'She took a mosey down the Labour to pick up her social security.' Judge Mason finds this slang, the language of the streets full of living quality, for, its origins unknown, it is often both onomatopoeic and evanescent – for example, 'not to worry,' 'no way,' and 'know what I mean?'

The Judge traces the subjunction of *wise* as in money-wise, effort-wise and talent-wise, in direct lineage to Chaucer. He wonders why it was suddenly resurrected, not by professors or leader writers, but by ordinary folk, during the 60s. He muses on buzz-words like 'smashed' or 'cut' meaning drunk or doing well, 'up for grabs,' 'hassle' and 'come-uppance.' Very often, it appears, newspeak comes from a new usage rather than a new word.

The language of the cells too, continues the Judge, has a drama all its own. For example *the blag was a doddle* (the robbery was easy) but it *all came over the top* (we were discovered) because one of our number *lost his bottle* or *spilled the beans* – when all we need have done was *tough it out*. The police, of course have a variety of names including *fuzz, pigs*, and *Old Bill* (to mention some of the more polite ones) some of which are used by the police themselves.

How long will such words last? asks His Honour. The quickest to die appear to be those devoted to the fair sex, e.g. the pre-war in-word *skirt* – how long are *dolly-bird* and *raver* likely to last? The prospects of recent contestants like *cobblers*, a mild term of abuse, *sharp* meaning smart, or *chipper* meaning cheerful are hard to assess. Courtly English in truth is vibrant and direct, not archaic and arcane, continues the Judge. His day was made by a defendant, in a case where the posting of a notice was in point, who said that 'the notice had not been conspicuated, so I consolidated a solicitor who told me it was a matter of the royal provocative, as a result of which I was held in gaol for twenty-four hours on superstition.'

 **BREAK ...**

Some 'gems' culled from radio and press during 1984.

Nick Ross on the subject of the Island of St. Helena: *'they have a good deal of money spent on them by we in England.'*

Newsreader: *'After seven days in custody, their case came before the magistrates to-day,'*

Roy Hattersley in *'The World at One'*: *'Simple column inches is not the criteria....'*

Brian Redhead to Sir Geoffrey Howe: *'... incurring much lesser costs ...'*

A discussion on travel: *'It sounds like vote-catching on behalf of* (instead of 'on the part of') *the Dutch government.'*

South-East News, 60 Minutes: *'The youngest of two brothers.'*

Pattie Coldwell in *'Rollercoaster'*: *'Here I am, sitting amidst these two obsessives ... '*

Twenty-four years down the line, and mistakes such as these are still appearing with great regularity.

IS THE AMERICAN ACCENT... ENGLISH?

Writing in *The Sunday Times*, Godfrey Smith recently asked 'Where does the American accent come from?' There is no easy answer. Robert Sinclar says: 'Simply listen to the sound of Gaelic in Donegal. There you will detect the authentic American sound.' Some say it started in East Anglia, while others relate it to Chaucer's Wife of Bath: *'Ful wel she song the service divyne/Entuned in hir nose ful semely.'* This mode, it is argued was adopted by the Pilgrim Fathers.

Patricia Tyrrell suggests that as Elizabethan words and phrases long obsolete in Britain still persist in remote areas of the USA, it may be that the Americans in their isolation kept the pure English accent, and that the present accent generally used in the United Kingdom may be a debased form of this.

Poul Høst-Madsen writes: I wrote two years ago in one of the publications of the Modersmal-Selskabet about the language of the BBC and the Voice of America (VOA) after visits to both institutions. I came to the conclusion that the BBC World Service excels in a beautiful Southern Standard English; but also that the VOA makes much more systematic efforts than the BBC in selecting and training newsreaders and is superior even to the BBC World Service in clear diction. This is in part because the monotonous American accent is easier to understand in short wave broadcasts than the English pitch …

TRANSLATION

Anne Shelley

Language forms part of any culture, and it has been said that translators are the mediators between one culture and another. Translations from Greek into Latin determined the beginnings of Roman literature; indeed, they have often led to the existence of, and development in, other cultures. Without translations of the classics there might well have been no world literature. Translators, then, can be said to carry literary wares from one culture to another in their capacity as custodians or trustees of a language. They can even enrich another language if they convey the meaning of the original into the second language well enough.

I should say here that I speak mostly from my experience as a translator from German though I have worked from French as well – usually a much easier language for the generally insular British to understand, partly because the word order is similar to our own.

There are three main axioms to be borne in mind if one is to communicate what the writer of the original wants to say simply and accurately: firstly, to translate the meaning, not just (sometimes not even) the words but to avoid the temptation to embellish because one thinks it might sound better. Then, ideally, one should never translate out of one's mother tongue, for it is rare that anyone has such a perfect knowledge of the other language that he can do this. It has often led to some misleading, funny, and at times hilariously ambiguous sentences in operating instructions or descriptions of a product or its manufacture when these have not been checked for accuracy; here I will quote one classic example that was not picked up before it was printed in a brochure. 'The entire bare body is moved into any number of positions by means of a pertinent fixture to apply underbody protection. For this reason, no overhead work is required and careful preservation is assured.' The reference was to the preparatory work done on car bodies before they were sprayed!

One should get away from the syntax of the foreign language and switch one's mind to that of one's own – in other words get far enough away to see the wood and the trees. One factor that is not given adequate consideration is that a wide knowledge of one's own language is essential: having a large vocabulary and being able to use it to advantage. This surely must include a knowledge of grammar – an aspect of language which I believe we in this Society all agree has been sorely neglected in our schools. I was rudely awakened to this fact while checking the work of some British students employed in Germany for some six months of their university career. While they were able to speak and write German fluently and accurately, they were often unable to construct grammatically correct English sentences, as I found when I pointed out to one young man that he had begun a sentence with an unrelated participle. After a moment's silence, with a puzzled look on his face, he asked what a participle was. How he ever learnt the complexities of German grammar I never found out, for learnt it has to be; though the most frequent cause of misunderstanding is not the sometimes clumsy form assumed by written and spoken German but rather the difficulty in determining what is actually being said. We have to translate the long encapsulated adjectival phrases as clauses, and try to keep them as simple as possible; by comparison, English sentence structure is somewhat simpler. Our language is derived from more widespread sources, with the result that we have a larger vocabulary; and clearly this means that sometimes there is more than one translation of any single German word, one of which may even resemble the German but may not be quite correct.

Then there is the 'register' into which one translates. There are basically three: the language structure required for political speeches, literature, scientific papers and so on, including official documents – and here one can fall into the trap of translating these into English 'officialese' – something which can ruin communication. Then there is the relaxed, less formal way such as one might find in newspapers and periodicals on subjects that do not require erudite literary prose, though some translators believe that this last can be achieved solely by using long words and involved sentences. Lastly there is dialogue, and here again one must get away from the idiosyncrasies of the original language; in the case of German, away from its sometimes excessive formality.

Dictionaries, of course, are essential and need to be chosen with care, balancing those compiled by nationals of the country whose language one is translating with those compiled by British experts or – better still – in collaboration one with the other. One needs access to first-class English dictionaries and also to *Roget's Thesaurus* – which I find indispensable.

Computer translations already exist in the commercial and technical worlds; that is to say, certain stock phrases used in commercial correspondence, together with the equivalent of a large card index of technical words and expressions, are already available. What effect will this have on language and how will people regard it? If it simplifies communication and speeds it up in these fields, all well and good; but I believe we are still a long way from computers which will be able to translate any literary, much less idiomatic, texts requiring careful selection of words, elegant construction, or the nuances and subtleties of English humour.

There is one modern problem to which Germany has adapted linguistically rather better than England – one aspect of women's liberation; for while we are still struggling with that non-word Ms, any woman in Germany can call herself Frau whether she is married or not, especially if she is over thirty – today Fräulein is used mostly by younger girls.

In conclusion, a word about interpreting, which is, after all, what translators do though here I am referring to the oral variety. One view, however, is that the stability of a language will be preserved in its written rather than its spoken form. Nonetheless, interpreting makes very heavy demands on the person doing it, particularly simultaneous interpreting (as opposed to consecutive) which today forms an essential part of United Nations and Euro-parliamentary procedure and of many international conferences as well. It requires several years' training, endless practice and complete control of one's nerves. I do not need to elaborate on the possible consequences of an interpreter making a mistake.

✳ ✳ ✳ *BREAK ...*

Lines from A Grandmother's Autograph Album

When the English tongue we speak
Why is 'break' not rhymed with 'freak'?
Will you tell me why it's true
We say 'sew' and likewise 'few'?
And the fashioner of verse
Cannot cap his 'horse' with 'worse'?
'Beard' sounds not the same as 'heard',
'Cord' is different from 'word';
'Cow' is cow, but 'low' is low;
'Shoe' is never rhymed with 'foe'.
Think of 'hose', and 'dose', and 'lose',
And of 'goose', and also 'choose'.
Think of 'comb', and 'tomb', and 'bomb',
'Doll' and 'roll', and 'home' and 'some'.
And since 'pay' is rhymed with 'say'
Why not 'paid' with 'said' I pray?
We have 'blood', and 'food', and 'good';
'Mould' is not pronounced like 'could'.
Wherefore 'done', and 'gone', and 'lone'?
Is there any reason known?
And in short it seems to me
Sounds and letters disagree.
... and here is another take on the same theme ...
I take it you already know
Of tough and bough and cough and dough?
Others may stumble, but not you,
On hiccough, thorough, lough and through?
Well done! And now you wish, perhaps,
To learn of less familiar traps?

Beware of heard, a dreadful word
That looks like beard and sounds like bird,
And dead: its said like bed, not bead -
For goodness sake don't call it 'deed'!
Watch out for meat and great and threat
(They rhyme with suite and straight and debt).

A moth is not a moth in mother
Nor both in bother, broth in brother,
And here is not a match for there
Nor dear and fear for bear and pear,
And then there's dose and rose and lose -
Just look them up – and goose and choose,
And cork and work and card and ward,
And font and front and word and sword,
And do and go, and thwart and cart -
Come, come, I've hardly made a start!
A dreadful language? Man alive,
I'd mastered it when I was five!

OPENING GAMBIT

To the amusement of my friends I once enrolled in an evening class to improve my powers of conversation. The teacher, a thin elderly lady had known everyone worth knowing and dropped names unashamedly. One of our lessons concerned the opening gambit – how to capture and hold your neighbours' attention at a dinner party, 'Be bold,' she said, 'and start with a riveting remark, for example: How are your tigers getting on? The effect of this may astonish you.'

This skill was well demonstrated to me some years later at a dinner party in New York. The guests included two Russians, who immediately took the floor and held it. They detailed the faults in their plumbing, the leaks in the roof, the difficulties experienced in getting builders to carry out repairs, the rascally ways of such people who only wished to exploit the public and so on and so on. How was the repetition of this boring saga to be ended. The other guests chewed on silently. Suddenly, a plump, blonde lady (who, we later learned, had escaped from Eastern Europe) interrupted the flow with the phrases, 'Have you ever stopped a lion in its tracks by tweaking its whiskers?' This electrifying remark quickly brought the rest of us back to life.

'Of course,' continued the blonde, 'I have always had big dogs, and you must, from the beginning, show them who is master.' Once, while she was staying in Brazil, she had heard a strange noise in the hall of the house in which she was staying. On investigation she found an unhappy lioness whispering in a cage. She immediately let her out! The creature it seems quickly realised who was in charge, and purring contentedly settled down at her liberator's feet. A beautiful friendship was soon established.

All went well until the animal's owner became jealous and forbade the blonde from associating with her dumb, four legged chum. Sometime later, however, the blonde discovered the creature standing over her owner, who was on the ground with her head almost in its jaws. A catastrophe was quickly averted when

the blonde lady stepped forward and seized her friends whiskers in the nick of time. The dinner party was saved too!

Come to think of it, if you ever want to get even with a crocodile, and have an arm free, you should punch him on the nose. It works!

ARE LANGUAGE ANCESTORS IMPORTANT?

F Shaw

Recent cogitations on the problems of past or present participle (I want the car *parked*, or I want it *parking*) raise the question of how far one may invoke Latin as a guide to usage in a Germanic language.

The tendency to make an appeal to Latin arises from the enormous number of words of Latin origin which we use. These words however are largely nouns, and while they vastly increase our vocabulary, they do not greatly affect usage. They are helpful and useful but they are not essential to the language. We can express ourselves using only Germanic words, but an English sentence using words only of Latin origin is an impossibility. Prepositions, articles, pronouns and auxiliary verbs all belong to the Germanic stock.

It is true that when we see a passage of Anglo-Saxon English, we find it difficult to realise that it is the same language as that which we use to-day. The difficulty is in the spelling, and in the uncomfortably unfamiliar shape of some of the letters. Hence we are inclined, for authority, to turn to Latin with its more familiar written aspect. But those who can cope with the pronunciation of Anglo-Saxon English claim that a passage of the prose of King Alfred's time will, if read aloud, still communicate its meaning to a modern listener. In print it may look like a foreign tongue, but the effect on the ear is that of our present day language. Furthermore, despite the influx of Latin words, it is probably true to say that four-fifths of the Alfredian vocabulary is still in use to-day. Perhaps as many as three words out of four in modern English are Germanic.

English is not a Latin language and Latin grammar is therefore a questionable authority in a decision on modern English usage.

✳ ✳ ✳ *BREAK ...*

The Wish of One Larry Burns

> In my dotage I've become
> Inert, defunct, inane.
> Oh, to be like yesteryear,
> Ert, funct and ane again!

THE SPREAD OF ENGLISH

SS Eustace

I recently chanced to turn on a television programme of three people conversing in a foreign language, which must have been Urdu, the language of Pakistan, unknown to me. I listened for seven minutes. In that time there were so many recognisably English words and phrases that I noted them. Here follow most of them (roughly in order of first occurrence): doctor, injection, specialist, sugar, general, individual, tablet, carbohydrate, high-fibre, fat, diabetic, diabetes, fruit, cheese, specially, enough, potatocs, problems, tea, control, test, instrument, blood sugar levels, prescriptions, needles, disposable syringes, infection, heart clinic, surgical spirit, jocolate (that's what it sounded like), Sorbitol, calories, suitable for diabetics, sugar-free, physical exercise, football, sandwiches, a thirty-gramme something, pancreas, insulin, programme, religious background. What were they discussing?

The programme shows how much English has penetrated Urdu as spoken in Great Britain, for they must have words for fat, fruit, enough, blood, thirty, etc. in Pakistan. The language there must rely on English less heavily.

Many loan-words indicate that a language is passing out of use, as is so with Welsh, Sorbian* or Canadian French. The anglicisms of European Urdu suggest that Urdu will one day cease to be spoken in Great Britain. Let us therefore, hope and assume that its future is assured in Pakistan.

* Sorbian, otherwise incorrectly called Wendish, is a Slavonic language very similar to Polish spoken decreasingly in Lusatia between Cottbus and Bautzen, east Germany, and in course of replacement by German. (There could yet be a cultural revival). Sorbian illustrates the point because it is already full of Germanisms.

TRYING TO TEACH SCIENTISTS TO SPELL

Dr Bernard Lamb

As a University of London lecturer with a hundred new students a year, I have an opportunity to influence the English usage of undergraduates. Although employed to teach Genetics, I feel that staff have wider responsibilities: we should aim to produce science graduates who are literate and numerate. At a minimum, they should be able to write clear, concise, correct English. Some of us were so appalled by current standards that we organised a College-wide seminar on 'What can we do about our UK students' use of English?'

I report here my own approach, which is very time-consuming, but the students will never learn unless someone points out their errors and ways of improvement. Any time I receive written work which can be returned (course tests, essays, practical books, but not examination scripts), I correct the spelling and grammar, but have to leave most punctuation errors just for reasons of time.

When students ask me if spelling matters, I show them examples from past exam answers where spelling errors have changed meanings, losing marks. It is all too easy to collect examples, such as confusions of effect/affect, infer/imply, compliment/

complement ('The two genes complimented each other …'!), thiamine (a vitamin)/thymine (a base), pistil (of a flower)/pistol ('This tomato variety has low fertility, due to a deformed pistol'), mediums (spiritualists)/media (mixtures for growing organisms on), past/passed, died/dyed, striped/stripped ('The female fruit fly has a more stripped abdomen than the male'), radiate/irradiate.

If I have a chance to discuss written work with a student, I try to give relevant spelling rules, a mnemonic, a derivation or some other positive way of remembering the correct version. To the 40% who write 'innoculate', I give the etymology from in (in) + oculus (eye, bud). To the 30% who write 'enviroment' (or many other misspellings of the word), I give the origin from environ (around) + ment (noun suffix). 'Abberant' (and its variants) are countered with ab (away from) + errare (wander).

Although it is no use expecting modern students to know Latin or Greek words, I always try to give etymologies of technical words in my lectures, as learning even a few common suffixes, prefixes and root words is a great help both with word meanings and spellings.

For the 50% who write 'occured', I give the useful but not well-known rule that if the stress in a two-syllable word is on the first syllable, you do not usually double the final consonant when adding to the word (fo-cus/focuses, proff-er/proffered, rabb-it /rabbiting). If the stress is on the second syllable, you usually double the final consonant (o-ccur/ occurrence, in-fer /inferred, remit/remitting). To deal with 'recieve', 'beleive', etc., I pass on the old rule about 'i before e except after c, if it rhymes with bee'. The last part deals with most of what would otherwise be exceptions, such as reign or feint.

Anyone putting 'normaly' is given the rule about making adverbs by adding -ly to the adjective, but some students do not even know the main parts of speech! Other common errors include prescence, independant, seperate, wheather, wether, and confusions between loose/lose, it/its and even where/were and their/there. It must surely be due to diminished reading and increased listening and viewing that one now finds some students confusing 'except' and 'accept', or 'whether' and 'weather'.

To deal with unclear handwriting, I show examples where confusion is likely, such as between wire, wine and urine, between amylose (starch) and amylase (an enzyme breaking down starch), painted and pointed. I point out many cases where 'd' is written exactly like 'cl' in their essays, turning 'dose' into 'close', for example. I ask them to consider how a typist would cope with unfamiliar names and technical terms in their writings. The inevitable response is, 'Yes, but you know what I mean.'

Often, I do not know what they mean, and I tell them that an examiner can not assume that some ambiguous or illegible word is necessarily the correct one. They are horrified at the idea that illegible or misspelled words could lose marks in an exam, as if that were malice on the examiner's part, not faults on the candidate's part. There was even a complaint at a staff/student committee meeting that I had 'marked essays for English not for science,' whereas I had marked for science, giving credit for accurate and clearly expressed facts and ideas, and had made constructive comments on the English, as this was one of the few occasions when I could help them to improve.

Correcting a scientific error could help with that one fact, but correcting their English could help them make a better impression in all subsequent exams, reports, job applications and even in private correspondence.

My main problem is that other staff rarely take such trouble (some have pretty shaky English themselves), so some students just think I am a crank. If only more staff gave our science students the same message about the importance of accurate and unambiguous English, it would be accepted more easily. If the schools did their job properly, teaching grammar and spelling thoroughly, with all teachers – whatever their subject – taking an active interest, then those in higher education could concentrate on higher education, instead of remedial English. Although I still make a lot of errors, my efforts to improve the students' use of language have at least helped me to improve my own imperfect standards!

UNITED WE STAND – DIVIDED WE FALL

The world-wide use of English is often cited as the main reason why the native speakers of English should not mind too much if our mother tongue is subjected to change. It is all in a good cause and we should be glad to share our heritage in this way. Our language does not belong to us, say some.

According to a recent article in the *Economist* however, Nigeria for example, nominally English speaking, has many language problems. While all government business, the Army and Police are all run in English, many Nigerians themselves find Nigerian English difficult to understand.

Nigeria has three main African languages, and some 300 others not so widely used. In the north, some 40 million speak Hausa, in the south-west about 20 millions speak the tonal language of Yoruba, while in the south-east 10 millions use Ibo. Street talk in Lagos is largely in pidgin, interlaced with Yoruba and Portuguese. Only a small group consisting of lawyers, civil servants, academics and business people use English for everyday purposes.

English is the sole language used throughout Nigerian schools. However, while the text-books are couched in English, the teachers who have to use them are often unable to speak it fluently themselves. Primary school pupils in the north are said to number 15 millions for whom sufficiently well-trained teachers are not available. Europeans are too expensive and other foreigners have not been a success.

The twenty Universities spend much time remedying the linguistic failures of the schools. Whereas the missionary schools in the south-east produce a good level of English, the Koranic schools in the north contribute to the growing divisions among the many cultures which are supposed to be united by English.

It is sad that English should suffer as a consequence of semi-illiteracy overseas.

✵✵✵ *BREAK ...*

Patrick Jubb

To be or to not be: that is the question.
Whether 'tis in the mind to nobly suffer
The split infinitives of ignorance
Or to adverbially take arms against them
To preposition them? to splice: to split:
No more: to ungrammatically say we end
The infinitive parting of unnatural shocks
That ignorance is heir to: 'tis a consummation
To devoutly be wished: no splice: no split:
No split? to perchance dream? ay, there's the nub.

NOUNS INTO ADJECTIVES

There is a habit that has become common among economists – and others – of using nouns excessively to qualify other nouns and suggests the rule to which Fowler would undoubtedly have nodded approvingly – that that if one must use a noun to modify a noun, one should use only one, or, at most two. He cites some examples of such abuses:

For example, in one manuscript, I found within a few pages of each other all the following: 'high risk flood plain lands,' which presumably means plain lands in which the risk of floods is high; 'aircraft speed class sequencing', which uses three nouns to modify a word that might be a noun if it existed but does not really exist; and then, to top it off, 'terminal traffic control program category'. There is no reason to obscure thought by using such elephantine language.

The article ends with a section called 'Grace and Force', which should be of great interest to all members of the Queen's English Society. After having dealt, at some length with the requirements of clarity, he adds:

Even if clarity should be our first aspiration, why not aspire to more – for example, to conciseness, force and, even, vividness?

Merely to achieve clarity one does not pay much attention to how easily prose reads, although the two qualities are related. Still, ease of reading does help the reader to retain his presumed original interest in a manuscript. You can take a long step toward making your manuscript not only clear but easy to read if you avoid using strings of nouns like those mentioned early in my remarks, and if you avoid fuzzy phrases such as 'In the area of' and 'in terms of.' If further you pay attention to how the words sound, you may even make the reading of the manuscript enjoyable. At a conference in Bellagio, someone asked Fritz Machlup (a prominent economist) why he had used one word in a draft rather than another longer one that the questioner found appropriate. Machlup said, 'Because it is more euphonious'. On being asked if he really paid much attention to that criterion when he wrote, he said, 'Absolutely, I ask myself – does it sing?'

After giving some examples of writing that pay little attention to ease of reading, the economist Walter Salant adds:

Another simple way of avoiding clumsiness is to prefer the short word to the long one and to avoid the unfamiliar word if a familiar one can be found that is equally correct, specific, and concrete ... That the length of words affects the cleanness and force of writing is not news. The powerful effect of short words hits one most forcibly in Ernest Hemingway's prose. His sentences strike like bullets. All are clear-cut and forceful. It is remarkable how many are built on words of one syllable.'

The author adds a statistical sample of the number of syllables used by Hemingway in *A Moveable Feast*, comparing it with that of three of the better writers among economists, whose writings are, of course, of a technical nature. Although all economists do not come out too badly, it is clear that Hemingway wins the prize. His score is that 83 percent of his words contain only one syllable and 96 percent one or two. He uses no words with more than three syllables.

To quote Salant's article: when words are not only long but general and abstract, the combination is deadly. The difference between such words and short, specific and concrete ones is strikingly brought out by George Orwell in his essay 'Politics and the English Language,' to which Herbert Morton, for many years the director of publications at Brookings, called my attention. Orwell quotes a passage from the Bible and then paraphrases it in what he calls 'modern English of the worst sort.' I shall reverse that order and give you his version first. You will probably not find it notable in any way because it is written in the style we read every day. Here it is in modern English:

Objective consideration of contemporary phenomena compels the conclusion that success or failure in competitive activities exhibits no tendency to be commensurate with innate capacity, but that a considerable element of the unpredictable must invariably be taken into account.

Now here, with a few introductory words omitted, is how the same idea is expressed in Ecclesiastes:

The race is not to the swift, nor the battle to the strong, neither yet bread to the wise, nor yet riches to men of understanding, nor yet favour to men of skill; but time and chance happeneth to them all.

If we all aspired to be Hemingways we should have to work at least as hard on our writing as he did. In *A Moveable Feast*, Hemingway said that it sometimes took him a whole morning to write a paragraph. When you read the book you will see why. Although it would be a poor use of resources for economists to spend so much time in polishing, it is obvious that many of us should spend a good deal more time in revising our drafts than we do now. None of us has the right, even at the stage of drafting to impose on others writing that does not meet the requirement of clarity. He who does so not only irritates his colleagues who must read what he writes, and wastes their time, but also forgoes the larger audience that might otherwise read what he has to say. He thereby forgoes the influence his work might have.

THE IMPORTANCE OF LEARNING ENGLISH GRAMMAR FOR THE STUDENT OF MODERN LANGUAGES

VJ Wrigley

Many teachers of Modem Languages must have wished that Primary School teachers and their English colleagues in the secondary schools had given their pupils some acquaintance with English grammar. I do not mean clause or column analysis, but feel strongly that it is not unreasonable to expect that a pupil arriving in secondary school should know the parts of speech and names of tenses and the difference between subject and object. They have, after all, had available the bulk of the teaching week in which to teach these useful and basic items of knowledge, while the language teacher will only have four or five periods a week in which to inculcate them, time which he needs to teach the language.

A great deal of the problem stems from the Colleges of Education whose staff have not passed on this information to the student teachers, who are themselves often sadly ignorant of grammar. University English courses have concentrated on Literature to the exclusion of a study of the basics of language.

Teachers at all levels could make use of the remaining inflections in English to teach the difference between a subject and an indirect case. Pupils who knew that even in English, it is necessary to use the object case of a pronoun after a preposition, and who therefore knew why *for we two* or *between you and I* are incorrect, would immediately find it easier to learn not to say *entre vous et je* or *zwischen er und ich*. If pupils learned when to use *who* and when *whom*, even more gains would accrue for instance in distinguishing between *qui* and *que* in French or *wer* and *wen, der* and *den* in German.

In Secondary Schools, the English teachers could at least mention the survival of the subjunctive in English. To someone who is used to saying *if it were true*, the German *wenn es wahr wäre*, would be easy, or if he knew why one says *it is essential that he be here at 1 pm*, the use of the subjunctive in French and Italian would be the sooner understood.

Above all, the essential seems to me to be that English children should know their parts of speech and names of tenses. Is it so difficult to learn that *I have + the past participle* is the perfect tense, that *I was eating* or *I used to eat* is the imperfect, that *bad* is an adjective and *badly* an adverb? At the least so much time would be saved in explanation. If, before one teaches how to form an adverb in French or Italian for instance, one has to explain what adjectives and adverbs are, so much time is lost.

There has been a philosophy among some English teachers that it is important not to correct mistakes in speaking or writing English, so long as the language is vivid. This has been harmful as the habit of accuracy is not learnt, and the teacher of languages is faced constantly with the infuriating question, 'Does it matter how it is spelt?'

Nor is grammar necessarily boring: it may be and can be a

pleasant change from so-called creative writing, comprehension or reading a book around the class.

The language teacher can return the help given by the English department in using examples from other languages to enrich the pupils' knowledge of English. A German teacher can paint the words such as *sore* in the Authorised Version equalling *sehr* (very); a French teacher can also use the Authorised Version to show that English too used the verb *to be* to make the perfect of verbs of motion (I am come that ye might have life): an Italian teacher would show that sentence inversion, common in Italian, can be used to vary the style (Other sheep I have) in English, too.

Modern Language courses at Universities are beginning to be less literature dominated. This should benefit the teaching of languages.

Since retiring from a Headship, I have taught adults occasionally in evening classes. They hope to be able to learn a foreign language in a course of one lesson a week, when they admit at the outset that they know nothing of grammar, yet they are too old to be taught as a small child might be taught. Several generations of school leavers have been tragically let down by their teachers. It is time all pupils had a better deal with a more academic approach to the teaching of English, so that we may cease to be a country which speaks no language accurately, not even our own.

WHAT PRICE CREATIVITY?

A partner in a national company of chartered accountants recently wrote to *Office Life* in long-hand. He has sought in vain to recruit a secretary who can spell. Of thirty girls recently interviewed, only half were able to type and only two could spell. For this situation he blames the schools for encouraging creative writing to the detriment of the basic tenets of English, grammar, punctuation and spelling.

Recruitment consultants bear out this deplorable state of affairs, and admit that many job applicants only score four out of ten in the spelling tests set. At the Anne Godden Secretarial College, the principal confirmed that the level of literacy amongst her students is much lower than in the past, when children could not have avoided learning to spell lists of words. Students now at the outset of their courses have to be taught basic English, which they should already have learnt at school. Pupils also fail in shorthand because they are unable to transcribe their notes. Many appear to have little interest, and, she believes, have been let down by the progressive methods in schools.

 *BREAK ...*

A HANDFUL OF HOWLERS

I saw the bridesmaids appear in their chauffeur-driven car, a lovely peach dress. The door opened to greet me, then I walked up the church to take my place in a pugh on the grooms side.

After all the guess were chauffeured to their seats the bride waltzed in with lovely long blonde hair which was plated. Her dress had a hooped skirt which was off-the-shoulder. She carried a boquet of red, white & blue carnations. With her dress swooping from shoulder to shoulder, the frill just covering her pale skin-coloured chest, she moved towards the groom her dress sliding across the floor. My chin dropped to the floor. The guests took their seats in the aisles and the music bellowed out from a rather fat lady on the organ.

One foot after the other they finally reached their destiny at the alter. The groom pulled back her vale and smiles & laughter stayed fixed in their faces as the vowels were sworn. The cannon smiles as his long cloth touches the floor. The people in their stalls were frilled although the brides mother, who wore a big white hat with netting across the top & a lovely peach boquet, got her hanky out with tears running down. Songs were sung & hymns were read as we sang 'Whilst Shepherds Watched.' The victor asked them to sign the registrar.

SIGNING THE REGISTRAR

After we had evaquated the church for the photograph ceremony outside, confetti was flown everywhere. Lots of photos were taken, many on their own. Brian and I stood in a couple of photos.

At the reception everyone queued up to kiss the groom. We sat down off course to a four coarse meal of turkey and chicken all set out on doyles. The main course was a roost with a baby chicken. I was hungary and the brides father in a smart 3-piece suite polished off his meal to a T. The bride had a three-tear wedding cake. The groom made a large speech and his aunt sang opera. There were three chandlers hinging from the ceiling. The disco went on till late and a good time was had by all.

Found by K Railton, an A-level examiner in English

IVE GOT A DEGREE IN LEISURE STUDIES!

A SMART 3·PIECE SUITE

 **BREAK ...**

EDUCATION ESTABLISHMENT ATTITUDES TO THE REINTRODUCTION OF GRAMMAR IN SCHOOLS
(With some help from Colonel Lovelace, 1618-1658)

There's no such thing as incorrect
One academic hints,
And mention grammar, I suspect
Progressive dons would wince.
It's trivial now to criticise
Mis-used apostrophes,
And teachers would be most unwise
To curb such liberties.

For tutors now – no doubt you knew -
Have ditched the triple 'Rs'
They have much better things to do
Than teaching kids to parse.
It's 'I' or 'me' as mood dictates,
From formal grammar free.
Oh, how those school illiterates
Enjoy such liberty.

Dry grammar don't a writer make
or rigid rules a sage.
A more creative stance we take
In this permissive age.
If there is freedom to mis-spell
And punctuation's free,
School leavers and trainees as well
Enjoy such anarchy.

AN ENGLISH LANGUAGE ACADEMY?

Elisabeth Barber

What happened in the 17th century was not that there grew up a public which demanded plainer prose, but that there accumulated a mass of information which demanded plainer prose. The men of science, when they did not write in clear Latin, felt they must write in clear English; in fact, the Royal Society did definitely demand plain and unadorned English from its members, as Thomas Spratt, the first historian of the Society, precisely records. In 1664, his colleagues gave effect to their views by appointing a committee for the improvement of the English language, which included, besides himself, Waller, Dryden and Evelyn. We have never come nearer than that to the foundation of an English Academy resembling that of the French.

The admirable John Wilkins (1614-1672), afterwards Bishop of Chester, one of the founders of the Royal Society and its first secretary, had recommended in his popular *Ecclesiastes, or the Gift of Preaching* that the style of the pulpit should be plain and without rhetorical flourishes. Stillingfleet preached in plain English, and South (1634-1716) not only preached in plain English, but mocked at those who did not.

The influence of France upon England in the 17th century was quite considerable. Though the Civil War checked for a time the French studies of Englishmen, it ultimately contributed to their diffusion; for it sent many English men-of-letters to Paris. In 1646, Hobbes, Waller, D'Avenant, Benham, Cowley and Evelyn were gathered together in the French capital.

In the later 18th century, the study of natural history, the establishment of museums and the advance of such studies as geology and marine biology (1765: founding of Kew Gardens; 1788: The Linnaean Society) all demanded a greater precision in the presentation of facts in plain English.

In the first half of the 17th century we meet with various devices to enrich literary style, exemplified, in verse, by the conceits of Donne and Crashawe and, in prose, by the antitheses and tropes of Bacon and the ornate splendour of Taylor, Milton and Browne. The Royal Society appointed a committee to improve the language; but nothing was done. What an academy could not do was done by a great writer, Dryden, who showed how great prose and great poetry could be written in a conversational manner.

Addison expressed a desire for 'something like an Academy that, by the best authorities and rules drawn from the analogy of languages, should settle all controversies between grammar and idiom'. Swift, more mistakenly, in his *Proposal for Correcting, Improving and Ascertaining the English Tongue* (1712), believed that there should be some method of 'ascertaining and fixing our language for ever.' Johnson, in the preface to his Dictionary, acknowledged with his usual manly sense that language was something not to be fixed by any lexicographer or academy, but urged the duty of individual responsibility in maintaining a high standard. A more recent invention by CK Ogden of what is called 'Basic English' reduces the number of essential words to 850, yet retaining normal English construction.

My comments: Swift would have been against change, but we know there must be change – increase of scientific knowledge, invention of word processors, mixing of immigrant population, even religious attitudes and freedoms which would do away with any kind of authority (when they don't bring God down to a common level) – and there will go on being change. But we want change for the better, not for the worse.

Could an Institute, an Academy or a Society possibly set out such guidelines as would preserve the best in all the changes that are bound to occur, and eschew all that undermines the richness and subtlety of the English language?

FOREIGN WORDS, MODERN & ANCIENT

David I Masson

All ordinary foreign words assimilated into English, and many foreign names, become 'naturalised' in their pronunciation in the course of time. What attitude should we take to this process? We must make up our minds about how it ought to proceed and what stage each given word should have reached.

The picture is complicated, if we take the past into account. Some names have actually altered their spelling (in some cases, via an intermediary language): *Aberdeen, Algiers, Athens, Barmouth, Calcutta, Carthage, Derry, Jerusalem, Lucknow, Moscow, Rome*, etc. Many ordinary words have also done so: *algebra, algorism* (from a personal name), *compound* (an enclosure), *crayfish, denim* (from 'de Nîmes'), *dollar, kyle, lariat, pidgin*, etc. We must face the truth: words have become anglicised by being mispronounced, slightly or grossly. They are often influenced by 'folk etymology', as in *Barmouth, crayfish, forlorn*, etc.; or by spelling pronunciation, as in *New Orleans, Rothschild, Van Straubenzee, Zinkeisen*. Other misinterpreted words include *indri* and *lariat* (this last from la reata, 'the re-tie').

Much of the original pronunciation has been lost for words such as *buffet, cafe, champagne, debris, garage, manoeuvre, Molyneux, muesli, reservoir, restaurant*; most are relatively recent accessions. With some speakers today, this stage has already been reached also (to my distaste) for *Cromagnon, debut, doyen, foyer, imbroglio, intaglio*. I can't so easily fault the all-the-way utterance of *garridge* (which has thus joined the Rothschilds and others.), the American *muss-tash*, climbers a*bb-sail* (from *abseilen*, 'to rope down'), or the military s*trayf* (from *strafe*, the imperative of *strafen*, 'to punish'); they are only following in the footsteps of *denim, guerrilla, hangar*, et al.

Recent names are quite another matter. *Braun, Löwenbräu, Porsche*, etc., have pandered to the ignorant, insular British, who utter *Zermatt* (i.e. 'at the meadow') to chime with 'sermon' and rhyme with 'fur-mat'. Yet contrariwise, *Majorca* now gets a y-sound, apparently in an effort to approximate to the -ll- of *Mallorca*; and people are frightened to speak of *Gaylic* today, compromising on *Guy-lic, Gallic* or *Garlic*. And there is ambiguity about *enclave, envelope, impasse*; for my money the first two at least should go all-English.

The slide into anglicisation cannot be stopped, though individual words resist varyingly, and Americans will probably go on accenting the last syllable of most French and Eastern words. Shall we in Britain, anyway, end up saying *baynal, ca-mufflidge*, etc., and perhaps even perpetrating spellings like *shovanist*? The drift could only be slowed down, a little, if we were to print foreign words and names in italics, and re-train speakers on the media. Meanwhile, I would hope that decent courtesy would be shown by everyone to genuinely foreign names, especially personal names, and that the titles of foreign works deserve a better shot at them than *Cozy fan tooty*. *Lohanbrow* should make us the laughing-stock of Europe.

In Classical words, names and phrases, once they are assimilated, i.e. excluding quotations and word-specimens newly lifted from ancient Greek and Latin, I advocate strict adherence to long-established habits (rules, if you like), which prevent us on the one hand from trying ineptly to imitate Latin or Greek, but on the other hand from procrusteanising a word into purely native English pronunciation rules or those for some irrelevant language. For heaven's sake, let it be understood that, in assimilated words and phrases, Classical *ae* and *oe*, while still so spelt, are sounded as *ee* (we don't want *essthete, alguy* or *ightiology*); Scots and Americans should be allowed *ay* for *ae*, and Scots the fricative kh-sound for *ch*, as in *loch*.

The ambiguous *eu* can be a trap, needing recourse to a lexicon or Classical dictionary. I don't like *feral* as *ferral*, which happens to offend both Latin quantity (often flouted anyway) and English habits; however, I do offend similarly by saying *morral* for *moral*, so I have to admit to irrational prejudice.

For words derived from Greek, we had best stick to the established (though anti-rational) antepenultimate stress, as in *-ology* words; thus in *diplodocus* the accent should fall on the first *o*, pronounced short. For words of Latin origin the stress pattern is more varied; and exceptions to the above are (chiefly) words ending in *-ic* and prefixes (such as *kilo-*) for positive and negative powers-of-ten of any unit.

But confusion has arisen through lax naturalisation of phrases over the centuries, e.g. *vice versa*, in Latin *wikkeh wairrsaa*, became *vighcy vurser*; now the second vowel has been dropped and all the original sense lost. Compare the idiocy of *ma-deeval* for *medi-aeval*.

 **BREAK ...**

Punctuation matters

> *Dear John,*
>
> *I want a man who knows what love is all about. You are generous, kind, thoughtful. People who are not like you admit to being useless and inferior. You have ruined me for other men. I yearn for you. I have no feelings whatsoever when we're apart. I can be forever happy – will you let me be yours?*
>
> *Gloria*

Dear John,

I want a man who knows what love is. All about you are generous, kind, thoughtful people who are not like you. Admit to being useless and inferior. You have ruined me. For other men, I yearn. For you, I have no feelings whatsoever. When we're apart, I can be forever happy. Will you let me be?

Yours, Gloria

THE PREGNANT PAUSE

Dr Bernard Lamb

My obvious aims in this short story are to intrigue, to amuse, to give pleasure. I also try to stimulate the readers' or hearers' interest in punctuation, parts of speech, types of noun, verb forms, etc. It has reminded some people of what they had almost forgotten, but were very pleased to find they could still recall, and has driven others – quite voluntarily – to look up terms in dictionaries and books on English.

Although it was written for an adult education class on creative writing, I have used it successfully with undergraduate and postgraduate scientists, whose general attitude is that any mention of grammar, spelling or punctuation is boring, insulting and unnecessary.

THE WRITER turned over in bed, torn between composing the next dramatic sentence of his novel and the subtler lures of sleep. Just as his subconscious formed the phrase: 'There was a pregnant pause …' his mind relaxed into sleep.

The thought was trapped where it was formed in his brain, deep in the word-generating convolutions of the cortex. Swiftly, the denizens of the verbal underworld pounced on it.

'Have you heard?' hissed the quotation mark.

'Heard what?' asked her partner at the other end.

'About the pause. The pause is pregnant!'

'Well! Well!' cried the exclamation mark. 'Whatever next!'

'What I'm in a terrible hurry to know,' panted the dash, 'is who did it – who's the wicked father-to-be?'

'You can stop looking at me,' said the dot dot dot. 'I'll admit I often insinuate, but I never inseminate. Maybe one of the parentheses did it ... They always seem to need a suitably curved partner.'

'You're asking for a punch up the bracket,' retorted the parenthesis. 'We need a suitable partner, yes, but no one could say a pause was a possible partner for a parenthesis. Anyway, how do you know that the pause is pregnant?'

'I can answer that,' replied the full stop, gravely. 'The pause missed her period twice, and that's a most serious matter.'

'Well, I didn't do it,' said the colon, 'I was feeling much too turgid when the pause must have conceived, though I feel a new man since my irrigation. It could have been the solidus who did it: we all know he has his inclinations.'

'You're doubly dotty to accuse me, colon,' replied the solidus, slashingly. 'After all, I'd only just had a stroke.'

'Yes, but stroking whom?' chipped in a kinky comma.

      up
'Look ^ there!' indicated the caret.

They looked – and saw that a question mark hung over them all.

'Which of you made the improper liaison?' it asked.

'Not I,' replied the ampersand, curling its curves tighter & hugging its tail. 'I was only briefly standing in for AND. Perhaps it was the hyphen – always trying to cut a bit of a dash & link up with anything in sight.'

'Thank you, but I'm a hyphen, not a lowphen,' came the dignified reply.

'I don't believe that any of us respectable punctuation marks would ravish a pause,' said the semicolon. 'After all, most of us put a stop to things or at least come in in the middle, we don't usually start things on our own. It's far more likely that one of those words did it.'

'It could have been the author,' someone suggested.

'The author?' gasped the punctuation marks. 'Who the hell's the author? What right has any brutal outsider got to make our poor little pause pregnant?'

'Can't I do what I like with you all?' asked the author, half waking.

'No!' they bellowed back in unison.

There was a pregnant pause...

COMMONSENSE GRAMMAR

Joseph Grindrod

As a retired teacher of English in a school which changed before my eyes from an all-boys municipal Grammar School into a gigantic Comprehensive, to me English grammar, with its terminology and technicalities, is as natural and sensible as the terms of anatomy in medicine or the rules in a game of football or snooker. I would as soon entrust a child of school age to a teacher of English, or any other language, who was not familiar with the parts of speech and their functions, as to a surgeon or dentist who did not know his parts of the body.

I say 'of school age', because I am perfectly aware that there is only one real teacher of language for the little child, and that is the mother. We all start to speak like our mothers. Then, when we begin to walk or kick a football Father takes a hand. By the time we mix with other children we 'know' the language, and our speech begins its long course of modification at the hands, or rather the voices, of our contemporaries and the numerous other influences that bombard our ears. Nowadays the dialects of the 'EastEnders' of London, the 'Neighbours' and the 'Young Doctors' of Sydney, and the inhabitants of 'Dallas' and 'Emmerdale' are equally familiar to our children and grandchildren even before they can write a word.

For the rest of our education, the process is to a greater or lesser degree remedial. This is why I make the analogy with medicine. I could also use that of car mechanics. We may drive for a long time without knowing what goes on under the bonnet; but when we cannot start on a frosty morning, somebody has to use the necessary technique. And nothing is more humiliating or time-wasting than going to the Unipart counter without being able to put a name to the part we want. Hence the necessity for parts of speech and, most important, an awareness of their functions in a sentence.

When formal grammar questions disappeared from O-level papers, together with any word that could be construed as a technicality of language, e.g. tense, superlative, preposition, a sigh of relief went through some sections of the teaching profession. And when Her Majesty's Inspectors began to whisper that detailed correction of a child's writing was discouraging and time-wasting, there was an almost audible cheer. The word was passed down to all levels, and it was not long before pupils were entering the first forms of secondary schools who saw the small print after dictionary definitions as so much gibberish; a teacher's appeals to use more expressive adjectives and adverbs were met with a blank stare.

The effects spread upwards. A-level English was confined to Literature, with a growing emphasis on content rather than technicalities of style. At college level, I suspect that lecturers soon found it unprofitable to talk of participial phrases or subordinate clauses, and budding English teachers were encouraged to think up more and more intimate situations on which their future pupils might express their innermost emotions. At university level, those English students who had managed to retain a knowledge of traditional grammar (often acquired from their Latin teachers or from underground grammarians like myself) could utilise it in the study of Old Norse or could abandon it for the new categories of the linguistic structuralists.

So we have the present state of affairs, in which the Oxford examining-board complains of 'grotesque errors of expression' in its A-level scripts. Yet the same board and its equivalents at other universities have combined to produce a new GCSE syllabus that still refuses to examine the technicalities of language, even of foreign languages. The latest report on the teaching of English in primary schools published under the chairmanship of no less a traditionalist than Professor Brian Cox concedes that Primary pupils should learn to recognise and understand nouns and verbs, but 'not in separate grammar-only lessons, and without learning by rote'.

So what can we do about it in a democratic society? I used to half-envy the Yugoslavs their dictator, Tito, who gave them a 30-letter phonetic alphabet by decree, thus solving all spelling-problems in the Serbo-Croat language at a stroke; but events since his death have shown the depths of animosity he aroused in the Serbian minority. Persuasion is the best in the long run, though time is not unlimited.

There might be plenty of teachers still around who could write out a scheme of grammar on the back of an envelope; but we are getting older all the time. The task is to persuade the university linguists either to agree on a new system of grammar, or to admit that the old system is still adequate to describe the English of today; to persuade the present generation of teachers to teach grammar in the classroom; and to persuade the DES and HM Inspectorate to insist on high standards of positive language-teaching.

✳ ✳ ✳ *BREAK ...*

CREATIVITY – Leslie Hook

To grammar I acknowledge my proclivity,
Which makes me someone trendy dons berate.
It's not that I'm opposed to creativity,
But rather what the grammarless create.

The current teaching-code seems sheer stupidity,
School-leavers swell the vast illiterate.
If these were taught grammatical lucidity,
We might learn what they're bursting to create.

Is teaching English grammar so elitist?
A view that some would doubt and I dispute;
For unsung Miltons need not be defeatist,
No more remain inglorious and mute.

ENGLISH 'AS SHE IS SPOKE' DOWN UNDER

M Chapman

It is always very easy to 'nit-pick' about the language of others around us. I am very conscious that my own leaves a lot to be desired and, what is worse, is deteriorating, but surely, the recognition of bad or idiosyncratic speech or writing in others at least means that we are aware of our own language. As far as I am concerned, one of the great delights of the English language is that it is so inconsistent, so full of nuances, and that it lays itself open to such manipulation.

I am fortunate that I live in Tasmania, where the language is still recognisable as English, and that I teach in an Independent (Private) School where speech is reasonably pure and where such anathemas as grammar and spelling are still taught. A Grade 3 classroom has a notice outside: 'We do not say YEAH in here.'

IT'S AWRIGHT SIR – I CAN TEACH IT YOU!"

Even here, however, enunciation is frequently poor. For instance, Australia-wide, the letter 'T' is fast disappearing, very obviously in such numbers as 'twenny' and words like 'plenny'; and generally it is becoming difficult to distinguish it. Possibly some reasons for the general slurring of the language are those suggested by Bill Homage in his book *The Australian Slanguage* – to wit, that it is the hot climate which leads to laziness, or (I love this one) that mouths have to be kept shut to keep the flies out. I would add that Americans keep their mouths closed, which is certainly another reason for the world-wide deterioration of clear speech. More serious than the 'T' is the emergence of an emphasis on the non-existent 'E' in words such as 'known'. We are treated, even on the ABC, to 'knowen', 'showen', 'throwen', and this is beginning to appear in spelling too.

Further on the subject of mishandling the language I must mention the Great Australian Haitch. This is, of course, the Irish influence. I left a Catholic School after ten years with a sigh of relief that I had managed never to say Haitch. That Haitch is ubiquitous: 'Haitch E C' (Hydro Electric Company), 'Haitch S C' (Higher School Certificate). Even the highest person in the land, who, of course, went to a Catholic School, is an exponent of the Haitch. I was informed by a new pupil, 'My name is Sarah, spelled with a Haitch.' As you may gather, the hackles rise on my spine whenever I hear that Haitch.

In our early days here the ABC provided pronunciation guides. It certainly does not today, being among the worst offenders, but it was refreshing to receive from a friend a booklet which is given to reporters on a mainland paper. The booklet is a very comprehensive guide to the English language. They are even forbidden to use such terms as 'chairperson', 'm/s', etc., so perhaps one day sanity may return. The local paper, too, stated recently that it would avoid the use of American spelling. The headlines next day were in American, but since then they seem to have acquired an English dictionary.

Mispronunciation can lead to some delightful pictures. What, for instance, is a 'triantular'? Naturally 'rhodendrums' grow very well out here, according to a gardening expert, among others. I wish that I could draw.

Australia is renowned for its 'mateship', its classless society. Fair enough (if it happens to be true), but do we also have to suffer the great diminution process? I do admit that I might have referred jokingly to 'bikkies' when the children were young, and certainly 'puppies'

TRIANTULARS

was a normal word; but not for every variety of canines, including geriatric Great Danes. Here we have 'puppies', 'doggies', 'barbies', 'vegies', 'chippies' and many more.

Another levelling-down process takes place with names. My husband invariably becomes Phil, though I, with equal constancy, introduce him by his full name. What is worse, the reverse process is also normal – Hughie, Gwennie, Petey, Johnno. I cannot leave names without a reference to double-barrelled names like Lee-anne, Su-ellen, Kerry-ann, Mary-lou, Justann (he is a boxer).

Grammatical construction is becoming a thing of the past. There is no doubt that George Orwell's Newspeak is no longer fiction. After all, one word must be more efficient than two or three. Watch/listen to television or radio and you will soon find that out. The other day, the ABC informed us that an area had been 'droughted'. 'Suicided', 'dialogued', 'partied' are normal. A well-known academic stated on an educational programme that the 'Artists had fleed to the suburbs'.

I'M OFF TO JOIN THE CIRCUS!

One of my particular *bêtes noires* is 'second-last'. I invariably ask the children how anyone can be behind the last person. The Headmaster insists on 'penultimate', which probably sails over most heads.

What do you think of 'The creation of … is an abortion'? It was probably true in that it referred to some government department. There was a wonderful picture conjured up by a feature writer in the local paper, who because of an electricity cut 'laid in bed in a semi-comatose state'. He wrote in a later article about a phantom egg thrower, with some clever punning, but apparently did not realise that he must have produced the eggs. Another news item stated that a man 'pleaded guilty to the mistreatment of a thousand sheep in the Magistrates Court.'

That is what I mean. You can have such fun with English.

A language must live, provided that all good language is not killed in the process, and Australian expressions are vivid and often enjoyable. What does 'Going on and on like a pork chop' mean? You have surely heard of 'Beyond the black stump,' 'like a stunned mullet,' 'within a bull's roar.' There are splendid anachronisms. The weather forecast states that it is 'presently raining' and robberies are carried out by 'bandits'.

I cannot resist one last comment. Perhaps it is because down here we are upside down, but I expect the same thing happens in England. I was taught to read from left to right and top to bottom, so I cannot make myself read signs painted on the road other than as:

ENTRY	**DOWN**	**TURN**
NO	**SLOW**	**RIGHT**
		NO

DOES ACCENT MATTER?

Michael Russell

A recent news item described how a Birmingham girl had been sacked from her job as a telephone receptionist because she was deemed to have too harsh a Brum accent even for a West Midlands firm.

This was picked up by Central TV as a topic for its Friday night LIVE show. QES was asked for a speaker and so I joined the audience in the Birmingham studio at 10.15 pm for half an hour of rumbustious discussion, led by Professor John Honey, author of the much-quoted *Does Accent Matter?*. He stated that surveys consistently showed that the accents most disliked, along with Scouse, Glasgow and Belfast, always included Brum, with its annoying whine. Instant outcry ensued, as expected – and required – from the audience, mostly of young locals.

My brief contribution made the points that 1) accent itself did not matter, so long as it did not hinder comprehension; 2) my own ear was hideously offended by Brum, much as a musicians is by bagpipes; 3) I had started life talking Sarf Lunnon, but had painlessly acquired RP as I went to grammar school. Those who found themselves working in a broader span of country than their home parish should try to lose – if this did not happen spontaneously – the harsher features of their original accent.

It seemed however, that Brum speakers were determined to hang on to their accent, at whatever cost; many were disgusted that anyone should dare to despise it and rebutted the notion that some amelioration was possible or acceptable – in a PC sense.

But even some of the locals disliked the sound of Brum – one girl said of her boyfriend: 'Oi ate ther way e speaks soomtoims – like "entcher" at the en v the sen'ence.'

[Note: a shudder-inducing rising cadence at the end of the statement is to be imagined.]

QES 'CANTPHRASE' COMPETITION

Here is the final selection of entries for the QES Cantphrase competition. Readers of QES News will recall that it called for three columns having five words apiece. By selecting any one word from each column, from left to right, one could construct a hundred and twenty-five phrases designed to inspire awe and feelings of inadequacy in the unwary (and uninformed) listener or reader.

For sociologists and economists (June Bassett, Amberley, West Sussex)

ONGOING	INSTITUTIONALISED	ANALYSIS
SUBSTANTIVE	JUDGEMENTAL	PARAMETERS
POSITIVE	COMPLEMENTARY	EQUATION
PLURALISTIC	SOCIO-ECONOMIC	SCENARIO
HOLISTIC	QUALITATIVE	AGENDA

For institutional/commercial use (Edward Deal, Somerset)

FLEXIBLE	ONGOING	SITUATION
CO-ORDINATED	BACK-TO-BACK	POTENTIAL
MULTI-FACETED	LATERAL	PERFORMANCE
FREE-FLOWING	UPDATED	SCENARIO
SECURE	MOTIVATED	ORGANISATION

For would-be new contributors to *Quest*: (M Hosier, Derby)

APPALLINGLY	AMERICANISED	BBC
DEPLORABLY	ILLITERATE	JOURNALISTS
DISMALLY	PROGRESSIVE	MEDIA
SADLY	SLOPPY	STANDARDS
TODAY'S	TRENDY	TEACHERS

[Mr Hosier's entry is not truly in the spirit of the competition since it provides intelligible phrases, but is included for amusement – Ed.]

✳ ✳ ✳ *BREAK ...*

A guide to pronunciation – Anon. (sent by Graham Carlisle)

Dearest creature in Creation,
Study English pronunciation.
I will teach you in my verse,
Sounds like corpse, corps, horse and worse.
I will keep you, Susy, busy,
Make your head with heat grow dizzy;
Tear in eye, your dress will tear,
So shall I! Oh, hear my prayer,
Just compare heart, beard and heard,
Dies and diet, lord and word.
Sword and sward, retain and Britain.
(Mind the latter how it's written).
Now I surely will not plague you
With such words as vague and ague,
But be careful how you speak,

Say break, steak, bleak and streak,
Cloven, over; how and low;
Script, receipt, shoe, poem, toe;
Friend and fiend; alive and live;
Liberty and library; heave and heaven;
Rachel, ache, moustache, eleven.
We say hallowed, but not allowed,
People, leopard; towed but vowed.
Mark the difference moreover
Between mover, plover, Dover;
Leaches, breeches; wise, precise,
Chalice, but police and lice;
Camel, constable, unstable,
Principle, disciple, label;
Petal, penal and canal.
Wait, surprise, plait, promise, pal;
Worm and storm; chaise, chaos, chair.
Senator, spectator, mayor;
Ivy, privy, famous, clamour.
And enamour rhymes with hammer.
River, rival, tomb, bomb, comb,
Doll and roll and some and home.
Stranger does not rhyme with anger,
Hear me say, devoid of trickery,
Daughter, laughter and Terpsichore,
Typhoid, measles, topsails, aisles,
Exiles, similes, reviles;
Scholar, vicar and cigar,
One, anemone; Balmoral,
Kitchen, lichen, laundry, laurel;
Gertrude, Germain, wind and mind;
Scene, Melpomene, mankind.
Billet does not sound like ballet,
Bouquet, wallet, mallet, chalet,
Blood and flood are not like food,
Nor is mould like should and would,
Viscous, viscount; load and broad,
Toward, to forward, to reward,
And your pronunciation's okay
When you correctly say croquet.

THE CAMPAIGN FOR REAL GRAMMAR

Michael Dummett

The English of grammar books is in retreat, attacked on all sides by jargon and obscurantism. Some seem content with the 'English language as she is spoke'. But Michael Dummett, Professor of Logic at Oxford, is determined not to let this sleeping dog lay. [sic]

Like everything else, even mountains, languages change. Unlike mountains, languages are human artifacts; we, their speakers, therefore determine in which respects they change and in which they do not. Many people's reaction to anyone's objecting to the use of a word or the syntax of a sentence is to say, you can't stop a language from changing, as if linguistic change were an external force beyond our control. This reaction, and others like it, have brought the English language to the verge of utter corruption. It ought to be obvious that some changes harm the language, while others enhance it, and that we should therefore resist the harmful ones and welcome those that are beneficial. A simple example of a harmful change was the repeated use by an eminent person in a recent interview on Channel 4 News of the word creditable to mean credible. (I forget who the eminent person was: I have become weary of making notes of all the errors I read and hear.) It is obvious that if this mistake becomes general, a useful word will have been needlessly lost to the language, with no compensating advantage: so such a change ought to be resisted.

It is, however, hard to persuade a great many people to resist mistakes, because their linguistic immune systems have, with purpose, been destroyed by what they were taught in school. A professor of cultural studies recently wrote to the *Independent* to say that it is in principle impossible for a native speaker to make a mistake, because the language simply consists in whatever native speakers say. It would be interesting to know at what age the professor believes that a child becomes in principle incapable of making a mistake.

The doctrine that there can be no such thing as a linguistic mistake has been transmitted by professors of linguistics and of education to the teachers; they have passed it on to their pupils, who have, naturally, absorbed it with a feeling of relief that they no longer have to bother about grammar or vocabulary. The doctrine is of course no more than a half-truth. A word does not bear its meaning on its face; nor does a syntactic construction bear on its face the relation imposed on the component words. We understand one another because we have learned the meanings of the words and the force of the constructions: without rules to govern it, a language cannot serve as an instrument of communication, and hence cannot survive. It is true that, when someone abuses the language, he will often (though by no means always) make himself understood, because his hearers guess correctly at the mistake he has made. It is also true that, if a mistake becomes sufficiently widespread, it will cease to be a mistake; semantic and syntactic rules are indeed not immutable. But the mistake was intelligible when it was first made because there were rules then in force about other words and constructions; we understand *creditable* when misused, because we know the word *credible*. There cannot be a language without grammar and without standard meanings; the only question is which rules we should maintain and which it will do no harm to abandon.

A language is a finely tuned instrument; it is a crime to damage it. To say it does not matter how you speak, as long as you convey your meaning, is like using a finely ground razor to cut a piece of rope on the premise that it does not matter as long as the rope is cut. Those who say this do not actually mean it: they would look askance at someone who said 'Me shop go' instead of 'I'm going to the shops,' although there would be little doubt about the meaning. All the same, our language is in a desperate state, when no less a person than the Prime Minister has ceased to blush for using *lay* when he means *lie*. Yet all is not lost, since there are many whose linguistic immune systems still function; what is needed is the courage to resist linguistic pollution. I recently published a little book called *Grammar and Style** and expected it to be lambasted from every side. To my surprise, it has been widely welcomed; there are evidently many who feel the same dismay as I do at how the language is currently used by journalists, broadcasters, politicians and, alas, many academics. The use of ambiguous constructions and hideous jargon promotes confused thought. It would be within the bounds of credibility to find that the recent academic study entitled *Gender-Related Book-Carrying Behaviour* reported by William Hartston in the *Independent* had been funded by a research council; but no research council would fund one called *How Men and Women Carry Books*.

Grammar and Style. Michael Dummett. Duckworth 1993.

THE ROLE OF THE WRITER

Ivan Butler

The role of the writer can be quite simply stated in one word – communication. This applies equally whether the purpose is to entertain, to inform, to persuade, to uplift – or even to deceive; whether the result is to be a detective story, an income tax form, a poem, a newspaper article, a serious work of scholarship – or an advertisement. It follows therefore that the single essential ingredient of the work is clarity – with elegance of style as a secondary consideration, which is generally dependent on the subject.

An ill-written sentence which causes a jolt in the reader's progress can destroy the very thread of communication which the writer is attempting to sustain. The loftiest and greatest speeches are useless if they cannot be heard; the same applies to written words if their meaning is not clear and unambiguous. This achieved, however, the most complicated sentence which may be necessary in writing on specialised or intricate subjects need present no difficulties, even to a moderately able reader. In addition to not being understood at all, the careless writer runs an even greater risk – that of being misunderstood.

Take some simple examples unfortunately common today, such as the substitution of *presently* for now or currently. This usage was obsolescent in the 16th century, and its revival in this dubious form is quite unnecessary.

Why, for instance, use disinterested (unbiased) when what is meant is uninterested, why fortuitous (by chance – either good or bad) when what is meant is fortunate; why enormity (monstrous wickedness or serious error) when what is meant is vastness or magnitude? Fraught by itself is meaningless: it means full of ... and the writer presumably means fraught with danger. Such misusage merely leaves the careless writer open to misunderstanding – and we are all guilty of this at times!

Dictionaries, sad to say, have to be approached with caution. They are records of usage and abusage, and thus not always reliable guides to good writing. To their credit, the *Concise Oxford Dictionary* and, in particular, the *Oxford American* now contain warnings. The *Concise* inserts a D to indicate a disputed (that is, degraded) usage; and the Oxford American uses such phrases as ... to be avoided by careful writers. (If one is a writer, surely one is always careful?)

As long ago as 1817, William Cobbett put the matter with admirable clarity and conciseness: Grammar, perfectly understood, enables us not only to express our meaning fully and clearly, but so to express it as to enable us to defy the ingenuity of man to give our words any other meaning than that which we ourselves intend to express. This, therefore, is a science of substantial utility.

It is often argued that English is a living language: indeed it is, and the role – the duty – of the writer is to ensure that it is not killed. That it can also be a beautiful language is yet another reason for its preservation.

✳ ✳ ✳ **BREAK ...**

Decoding – Leslie A Hook
A diatribe directed to some modern poetry by an
amateur poet-manqué

The cognoscenti, who should know,
Regard my poetry de trop
And doggerel out-moded.
But is my writing any worse
Than highly obfuscated verse
That has to be decoded?

Too many poets of today
Deem it sufficient to display
Verse imagery-loaded
Which, if obscure, is not ideal
And lacks all meaning and appeal
Until it is decoded.

When punctuation's minimal
And sometimes isn't there at all
And syntax is eroded,
Small wonder readers shun the bard
Who makes their comprehension hard
With verse to be decoded.

Our William Shakespeare – and you know
He wrote four hundred years ago –
Gives instant pleasure, so did
Bards of his time, yet Laureate Hughes
Produces enigmatic clues
That have to be decoded.

If I should brusquely intervene
It all depends on what you mean
As once Professor Joad did.
Some avant-garde-ist might retort

Use your imaginative thought
And get the verse decoded.

But please no verse of gimmickry
That's shrouded in complexity
With readers incommoded,
But make it lucid, if you can,
Not like a secret army plan,
A mystery till decoded.

TALES OUT OF SCHOOL

Roger Poole

In this article I hope to reveal what goes on in teaching as I have experienced it in a career which spans four decades and which, even now, has not quite trickled to a standstill.

On one occasion I was speaking to a parent about the progress of her daughter who was shortly to begin her GCSE year, though she was not to be in one of my classes. I reminded the mother that for the first time there was to be no examination at the end as the English syllabus was to be validated by 100% course work. Yes, I know, replied the mother, and I shall make it my personal business to see that every bit of her course work earns a high grade.

Naturally, contributors to *Quest* are very interested in the use of English, and it is gratifying to know that we have so many defenders of the faith. Yet I do not think that this awareness and this concern are reflected elsewhere as widely as they ought to be, even amongst teachers. Of course, I know only too well that many teachers are dedicated, thoughtful, hardworking people, and that some are gifted. Even so, the written work I have seen of school pupils, of students in further education, and of pupils and students referred to me privately, suggests that something is wrong somewhere; it appears to me that a gap exists between what is and what ought to be.

As a further example I can instance a class of A level students, mostly aged between 20 and 40. (I have to add here that this kind of student deserves particular praise, since numbers of them, particularly the mothers, may have to deal with a wide range of domestic problems.) No teacher would expect their students of A level English to have a profound awareness of life and literature; I myself would be satisfied with a modicum, but it is disappointing to find there are whole echelons of a nation's culture the existence of which remains unsuspected.

I do not think the answer is to make A level English more popular or more relevant, as the jargon has it. I can remember one A level class where not one single student had heard of the parables of the Good Samaritan or the Prodigal Son. (All these instances refer to students whose culture was traditional and Western.) I have even had some students who had never heard of Adam and Eve, and plenty who had not heard of St Paul, Milton, Keats, Gladstone, Lloyd George, Clement Attlee, Harold Macmillan or Harold Wilson – and the list could easily be much extended.

Winston Churchill's name was well known, but many could not date him to within 50 years of his birth and many were surprised to know he had anything to do with the First World War. Napoleon, however, was no more than a misty name from a foggy past. The American Civil War was a quite unknown entity while the English Civil War conjured up nothing more than a melange of plodding Roundheads and dashing Cavaliers. To come to more recent times, even the major figures, Darwin, Marx, and Freud, were by no means known to everyone, and were confounded by some. The terms High Church and Low Church had no meaning for anyone. Happily the beacon of 1066 was still there in the distance, behind which the figure of King Alfred could be glimpsed, burning his cakes.

One year, I decided to attempt John Fowles's *The French*

Lieutenant's Woman. Apparently I had a good start here because the students liked the choice and half had seen the film. The drawback was that the film kept to the romance of the love story whereas the book delves a good deal more deeply. Anybody who is familiar with the novel will appreciate that it is packed with references and allusions, more prolific, if less esoteric, than those in TS Eliot's *The Waste Land*.

Rather than try to summarise these in detail, I will confine myself to saying that there are 100 or more references to people in history alone, and many to movements, philosophies, and events. The vocabulary is often demanding (e.g. aleatory, draconian, vulpine), and there is an infusion of foreign phrases, mainly French and Latin.

Now, I will not go so far as to say that not a single student ever understood one of the references, but such a statement would not represent much of an exaggeration. Nevertheless, the students enjoyed the book and gained from the encounter. Of course, we had to spend more time over it than otherwise we would have done, so that in this sense some time was wasted.

In general, it seems to me that at all levels of teaching we suffer from a lack of a common currency and that in schools, to my way of thinking, we need to spend more time on what I would call the fundamentals of language and literature.

It is all very well for some educationists to say that we should start with the child's own interests. Unfortunately, if we do, we may find it a very long journey from there to where we want them to be. There are a few who say we should stay with the child's own interests, and not seek to impose our own targets; but I do not think that many would accept that position.

If the faces of our older students shine with no glimmer of response when a famous passage from Kipling's *If...* or Shakespeare's *Hamlet* is quoted, is not something wrong somewhere?

THE TROUBLE WITH RELATIVES

Nicholas Bagnall

Every letters editor knows that there are three subjects that can be relied on to get the readers going: religion, animals – and grammar. Not long ago I wrote a fairly unprovocative piece in which I defended among other things the split infinitive and the disjunctive adverb (as in 'hopefully I won't be late'). The hate mail was fiercer than ever. Acceptance of split infinitives and of incorrect use of hopefully is trendy nonsense, wrote M D Tomlin of Blisworth. But it is par for the course in this second-rate country where standards are slipping all round.

Why do these things generate so much steam? The obsession is not new: Jonathan Swift was complaining about our defective grammar even in 1712. David Crystal, author of the *Cambridge Encyclopedia of the English Language*, got thousands of letters when he asked listeners to a Radio 4 programme to name their pet grammatical hates. He tells us that those who mentioned their age were mostly over 50. Swift was well into middle age when he wrote his *A Proposal for Correcting, Improving and Ascertaining the English Tongue*. William Cobbett's *English Grammar* was the work of a 66-year-old, and Bishop Robert Lowth was over 50 when he wrote his pettifogging *Short Introduction to English Grammar* in 1762.

Prof Crystal's encyclopedia gives examples of Lowth's rules. Never end a sentence with a preposition. Don't say Who did you speak to? – say whom. But the interesting point about Lowth is the reason he gave for his rules. The placing of the Preposition before the Relative, he explained, is more graceful, as well as more perspicuous, and agrees much better with the solemn and elevated style.

Generations of schoolteachers, desperate to interest their pupils in the distasteful subject, used to tell them they must learn it so as to avoid misunderstanding and assist clarity of expression. But there is no difference in meaning between, 'For which team are you playing?' and 'Which team are you playing for?' The placing of the preposition before the relative has nothing to do with clarity. It has much to do with manners – social convention and class. Cobbett, disgusted on hearing the Speaker of the House of Commons refer to 'subjects more various than are usually submitted' (it should of course have been 'than those which are usually submitted'), was not complaining that he hadn't understood what the Speaker meant. His objection was that chamber-maids write in this way and that something better was expected from the Speaker.

Angry letter-writers could do wonders for their blood pressure with a browse through Prof Crystal's book. They would learn that our grammar has been gradually changing all the time. The biggest change was in the 12th century, when we began to drop so many of the old inflexions which, as in Latin, had determined meaning and to depend more on word order. One theory is that the Anglo-Saxons way of talking was responsible for this because we tended to gabble the endings.

I must warn those who bang on about the decay of our language that the book may irritate them. This is because of the frantically jolly way in which Prof Crystal and the Cambridge University Press have found it necessary to present the material. For example, a section about the 12th-century Peterborough Chronicle is illustrated by a facsimile from the beautiful MS in the Bodleian.

But this is not enough for the editor, he feels he must put in a colour picture of the west end of Peterborough Cathedral as well, though it was built more than a century later.

It is as though linguistics were too tricky a subject to be served ungarnished. But this is not the real reason for all that decoration. It is that so many schoolchildren, now grown up, have been taught badly, have been put off the subject and need to be seduced back. But the scene has changed for the better. Linguists are less interested now in grammar, much more interested in semantics – the study of the meaning of words and their contexts. And, as Orwell knew, this matters rather more than the disjunctive adverb and the placing of the preposition.

 **BREAK ...**

Spellbound

I have a spelling checker,
It came with my PC;
It plane lee marx four my revue
Miss steaks eye can knot sea.
Aye ran this poem threw it,
I'm shore your pleas two no,
Its let her perfect in its weigh,
My cheque her toll me sew.

To rite with care is such a feet,
Of witch won should bee proud.
And wee mussed dew the best we can,
Cos floors are knot aloud.
Sow ewe can sea why aye do prays
Such soft where four pea seas,
And why I brake in two averse
My reed erse two a pease.

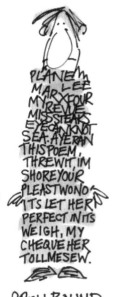

MIGHT BE RIGHT OR MAY BE WRONG

Fritz Spiegl

I return to a problem I have mentioned before, when it was no bigger than that biblical cloud the size of a man's hand. It has now grown alarmingly and often obfuscates the meaning of otherwise sensible statements. I refer to the difference between *might* and *may*.

When used in present-tense or in implied-future applications the two are often interchangeable, though with subtle differences, for

95

example that between I *might* speak to her and I *may* speak to her.

When one mentions something that is in the past, the two meanings diverge sharply – the difference between something that might have happened, i.e. the speaker is unsure whether it did or not (He might have walked along this path), or something that might have happened had a certain condition been met: Had he studied more he might have passed his exam, implying that he was lazy and did not pass. On the other hand, He may have passed his exam means that the speaker does not (yet) know whether he did or did not pass. What you cannot say is: Had he studied more he may have passed.

David Crystal's *Cambridge Encyclopaedia of the English Language* seems not to mention the might/may problem (certainly not in the index). Godfrey Howard's *The Good English Guide* (Macmillan) is more helpful, but says that the meanings express such fine shades of uncertainty and doubt, politeness and deference, that we need a chart to guide us as to what was intended.

There are also shades of hesitancy – the difference between, say, 'May I have a word with you?' and the possibly wheedling 'Might I have a word with you?' Howard has 'It might rain' and 'It may rain' – two slightly different statements.

Take the following examples (from radio, TV and the papers). I mention names (where I can) not to point out errors but to invite the distinguished authors to explain how they feel about them.

Angela Phillips in the *Independent*: *Had Virginia been at university today ... she may never have become a Bottomley ...* Is Miss Phillips doubting that Mrs Bottomley married Mr Bottomley? We know she did. There is no may about it.

Stephen Cape on BBC TV News about a stranded catamaran from which all passengers were rescued: *Some passengers may not have survived.* But as he said a moment earlier, all were taken off safely and all survived. Is he suggesting now that some did drown after all?

Hilary Finch in *The Times* about a concert: *Norrington may have done better to remind himself of Mahler's own declaration that metronome marks were inadequate ...* The critic postulates the possibility that Norrington followed Mahler's declaration, though what she means is that he did not, but ought to have done.

A BBC reporter whose name I did not catch: *A number of [jail] suicides may have been avoided.* The man had just told us about jail suicides that had happened and were not therefore 'may have been avoided.'

A very young Radio 4 reporter (who sounded as if she had inadvertently been left behind after the BBC's Take Your Daughter to Work day): *Had there been a proper search, the bomb on the [Lockerbie] airliner may have been detected.* The whole world knows it was not detected and of the consequent tragic outcome.

In each of the examples given, *may* should have been *might*. There is not an iota of doubt about it nor any argument; until a few years ago the writers would all, without question, have put *might*.

But suddenly this crazy habit has arisen of saying *may* instead of *might* and has spread through the media. *May* doesn't save time, sounds no better and conveys a different sense from that intended. It is not an elegant variation of *might*.

Many readers have complained that they find the confusion annoying. It is a perfect example of the way English can be learned only by feeling and instinct, and that often the only rule is there is no rule. Is the usage suddenly being changed? Is it American? I am flummoxed.

MIND YOUR LANGUAGE

Dot Wordsworth

A reader from Frome has asked me to consider the only serious defect in the language: the lack of a unisex pronoun. To avoid saving *he or she*, *his or her*, or *him or her*, recourse has to be had to the ghastly solecisms *they, their* or *them*.

I admit we are in trouble, just as we are over *who/whom*, the use of many pronouns and of *like* (which I can't seem to be able to get into some elementary-school pedants' heads). Not so long ago, *he, his* and *him* did not sound out of place: now apparently they do. But what is wrong with the *they* solution? An Oxford dictionary opines that some people think it erroneous, but some people are easily offended. It is all very well saying that 'they' is a plural, but just consider the strange history of a parallel development in the opposite direction, with the word *one*.

The 23rd sense of *one* in the OED is when it is added after demonstrative and pronomial adjectives and in the sense of a thing or person. Fair enough. The surprising thing is that *one*, surely a most singular word, has a plural form, *ones*; as in, 'Which sweeties do you like?' 'The red ones.'

This usage predates Shakespeare. Its ancient pedigree goes back to before the time that the word acquired a *w* in its pronunciation, which explains the regional or colloquial forms *biguns*, etc. A citation from 1587 has: *Let vs see what maner a* [kind of] *ones they be* (which also displays a nice appreciation of the subjunctive). The great Bishop Butler wrote in his *Analogy of Religion* (1736): *The three angles of a triangle are equal to two right ones*. So if one can form a plural, why can't a plural from such as they have a singular meaning? We need a common pronoun; they is already in use: there is no stopping it. If anyone dislikes it, they'll just have to lump it.

A WORD TO THE WISE

Adrian Williams

The draft of my first report as a management consultant was returned with (accurate) annotations, such as Rubbish, weak, poorly argued … I also recall the critique which began: Page one, line one, word seven: perhaps should, instead of will?

These two experiences, and many more over the years, have helped me to develop a style of effective business writing – and of effective criticism, too. I have noticed that there are a number of factors that affect the reader's judgement. These form two clusters: the objective factors and the subjective ones.

The objective factors are those which it would be sterile to have a debate about: proof-reading, spelling, grammar, or the correct usage of words. I will brook no debate about the correct use of 'disinterested' as distinct from 'uninterested', because I can carry my point at once by going to to a dictionary.

The subjective factors, by contrast, give us fertile ground for argument. Is the point well expressed, and hence clear? Would it have been better made if the whole structure had been different? Whatever the merits of the case made, does the writer's style meet the expectations of the reader? There are no rights or wrongs on these matters; the writer has to sift such criticism as he can organise for himself.

An analysis of the text is a good first step: a simple assessment of the strengths of a piece of writing, and of those aspects needing improvement. This is best done analytically, and in a prescribed order. It would be tedious to list all the factors that I use; anyone who is interested in my working checklist is welcome ask me for it.

Suffice it to say here that my first step, when I am asked to give a critique of a piece of writing, is to read it straight through, marking those points which are wrong by reference to the objective factors and making corrections as I go. This process gets rid of the distractions. I can then concentrate on the subjective factors, culminating in the all-important question: does this piece of writing meet the need?

A colleague once said to me, straight-faced, 'You know, Adrian, clients aren't bothered by trivia such as proof-reading or punctuation. It's the deeper issues they're concerned with: our clarity of thought, the authority of our argument, our originality, the confident expression of our views.' I didn't agree then, and I still don't. For I have been a client as well as a consultant.

I have received reports telling me about a number of MP's; people have promised to appraise me of the outcome, or have offered me the one criteria for successful demand-lead marketing; they have indentified key benchmarks form which I can guage the outcome; and they have called me Adrain Willijams in the Mangement Summary.

So I am in a position to say that trivial mistakes such as these (there are ten in the previous paragraph) are enough to make a client wonder whether an investment in a particular consultant has been well made. If you can't trust them on trivial matters such as spelling, how can you on the more profound issues?

Most business writers are actually pretty good on grammar and syntax. We can write sentences with verbs in them. We don't write singular verbs with plural nouns or vice versa. Business writers' problems with grammar usually come from a lack of control following the temptation to construct too elaborate a sentence.

The dangling participle is a common feature, of which my favourite example is, Having completed the assignment, the pigs can return to their usual winter quarters. Yes, of course I know what was meant, but the grotesque image fatally distracts my attention.

Punctuation is much more of a blind spot for business writers. Hyphenation causes problems – particularly to writers on technical subjects, who assail their readers with batteries of unconnected nouns used as adjectives, thus: The Department has imposed a large vehicle fleet operator mileage restriction.

Commas and apostrophes are poorly dealt with, too. Yet the rules of correct usage are easy to find, and apply. It's a pity that good punctuation is not well regarded as a useful discipline, since carelessness can damage the writer's message: gauge the effect of removing the commas in 'Consultants, who are known to be incompetent, should not be allowed to practise.' Good punctuation is like the dynamic markings in a piece of music: while the piece might stand on its own without them, the additional information is a courtesy offered to the reader to help him on his way.

My reason for dwelling on the objective factors is that the reader forms his first impression from them rather than from the important messages that are conveyed by the subjective ones. It is the content of the objective factors that contributes most heavily to the Exasperation Index: that percentage unread when the client decides to bin the document. I have experienced indices as high as 85 per cent; anything more than nil is a disgrace.

A consultant should have no difficulty in mastering the subjective factors concerned with content, structure, and power of argument. They are the explicit part of our unique approach. We fall down badly, though, in power of expression – the form of words that we choose to express our thoughts. Here, the message is one of liberation. As business writers, we have become stifled by sterile conventions.

For example, we were all told years ago that we shouldn't begin sentences with *and* or *but* – so we write tortuously long sentences instead. There is no grammatical foundation to this taboo, which is commonly ignored by writers from Gibbon to Enoch Powell; the *Financial Times* editorial page generally has half-a-dozen examples in each issue, though few readers will notice them. That's an important point: we are inhibited by baseless conventions whose breach we don't even notice.

Likewise, a fear of terminal prepositions makes us write 'Supplies are exhausted' instead of 'Supplies have run out.' We use 'It is recommended', rather than 'We recommend', because we have been schooled to think that the intrusion of personality is bad form. We use tired words and phrases because they are safe: we identify key issues, we commence new initiatives and we exploit the strategic potential of innovative opportunities. No wonder our readers sometimes find us tedious.

And does this matter? Yes, if the recommendations we make are so hard to unpick from the undergrowth of verbiage that our clients can't understand them. Yes, if our clients' spirits droop as they open up the awaited report and groan, 'Oh hell – it's double-sided.' Yet the remedy is simple, if we can but unloose the corset of convention.

There are many factors in the obstacle course before the reader can make a judgement, consciously or otherwise, on the all-important question: Does it meet the need? To make sure they get their message across, writers have only to write down the reader's need in ten words or so, and to check progress against their text from time to time during the course of production.

Many of the remarks I have made are not new: George Orwell can claim the credit for some of them. The odd thing is, we all know about correct spelling and not using the passive voice and preferring short words to long ones – but we often write as if we are immune from the need to practise those principles ourselves.

Take note – you never know which of the factors might let you down – excellence in all of them is the only safe way!

❈ ❈ ❈ *BREAK ...*

The QES Member – PG Tucker

I am the very model of a literate Grammarian,
I've studied Teuton languages, Low German and Bavarian,
Over Latin, Greek and Sanskrit I've spent many hours of
    study
But despite my loads of learning I am not a fuddy-duddy.
I will keep a participle, detached or fused or otherwise
And many split infinitives I'm very keen to authorise
And I know all kinds of pronouns – reflexive, relative or not
I'm familiar with the colon, comma, hyphen, dash and dot.

I can spot a double negative, a simile or metaphor,
I know a dozen idioms a common phrase is better for.
I love a lengthy conference, grammatical, syntactical
In the niceties of English, theoretical and practical,
I am very good at parsing, analysis and synthesis
I'm clear about the uses of both bathos and antithesis.

     But...
If I hear a catachresis in a statement on the air
I will crease myself with laughter or be driven to despair.
If I spot a nasty error, grammatic or semantical
I risk the wrath of foes and friends by being too pedantical
In righteous rage I write to *Quest* a letter periphrastic
Deploring English standards, written, verbal or scholastic
For I am the very model of a literate Grammarian
And cannot stomach English from an ignorant barbarian.

AGAINST ANTI-AMERICANISMS

Michael Gorman

One of our members recently resigned; he complained that we were not sufficiently firm in opposing instances of American usage, and he was tired of hearing the cliché, a living language is subject to change. I felt moved to reply to him, and the relevant points from that reply now follow.

I must contradict your first claim, that the English language arose in England. Nobody in Roman Britain spoke English. The Angles, Saxons and Jutes who invaded post-Roman Britain spoke Englisc, and proceeded to form the kingdoms of Mercia, Wessex, etc. These lands and peoples became known as Anglecynn; but it was not until about the year 1000 that the name England came into use. So it is the language which gave its name to this corner of our island, and not vice versa.

The English language has progressed to become a world language, and I feel pleased and privileged to be one of its users. Because of its world status, I consider it wrong to take a narrow, nationalistic view of it, and I will not support a blind, anti-American attitude.

The language has borrowed enormously over the centuries, but has discarded nearly as much, and is immensely richer as a result. This brings me to the topic of change in the language. I feel uneasy when I hear people say that a living language is subject to change. Our friends, it seems to me, use it as a glib phrase without really understanding it; they do not want to be labelled as fuddy-duddies for opposing all change and so they recite the words in order to appear enlightened, but firm.

Our enemies, on the other hand, use it as an excuse to get away with anything. Change is the result of two separate processes. There is the introduction of new words and phrases into the language in an unpredictable way, as people search for new ways to express their thoughts. There is also the vanishing of words and phrases for reasons which are much more apparent. As examples, outdated words for outdated products fall into disuse, fashionable words fall out of fashion, and foreign words are altered to fit the sounds and rhythms of English.

By understanding such processes as these, the QES can help to kick a word while it is down, as a part of our aims in encouraging clear and pleasant English – the awful *gung-ho* and *second-guess* do seem to be on their way out. But ugliness should be attacked because it is ugly, not because it is American.

Sloppiness in public English is as much bad manners as sloppiness in public dress or public eating. But although I so strongly dislike the word, it is difficult to think of an equivalent to *second-guess* without clumsy circumlocution; the same goes for *hopefully* at the beginning of a sentence.

Maybe some constructions will turn up to patch these holes in the fabric of our language. I shall form my own opinion of them if they do.

TALES OUT OF SCHOOL – THE STATE WE'RE IN

Roger Poole

This article concludes with a verbatim copy of a piece of work by a boy of 15. This pupil is in the 4th year of his secondary school career, which means that he has ten years of education behind him, and that he will be sitting his GCSE English examination in the following June.

He was referred to me by his parents because they felt his school was unable to help him in any satisfactory way. They were concerned about his English in general but particularly about his inability to punctuate. To assess his ability I asked them to get him to write for me a story which included a good deal of dialogue, but which also contained some description of people or places.

It is fair to assume that readers can write English well and that they are concerned about the state of English and the way it is taught in this country. Yet, because of their high level of attainment, it may be that they are insulated to some degree from the true situation that pertains in our schools.

I have spent some time in recent years in further education and in the private teaching of individual children and young people mostly between the ages of 14 and 18. The result is that I have first hand knowledge of their attainments. I know what they tell me, I know what they write for me, and I know what they write in school.

What they tell me alarms me, and what they write in school is often inadequate and weak. It is only a slight exaggeration to say that I look for excitement and colour but find none; that I look for accuracy but encounter faults and laxity; that I look for knowledge but seek it in vain.

There have been periods in our educational history when teachers taught grammar, word knowledge and writing techniques; there have been periods when the emphasis was on feeling and creativity and on the inspirational use of literature; now I find little evidence of either. I remember very well one A-level English literature student who knew nothing about either figurative language or the use of form and stress in poetry. I have known dozens of A-level English literature students whose knowledge of major figures in history or in our culture was limited to only a few names, such as Jesus Christ, William the Conqueror and Sir Winston Churchill.

I have met some such students who had never heard of Adam and Eve, the Prodigal Son or the Good Samaritan, and I refer to students brought up in our native culture and not to those whose roots were put down in other soils. I remember a girl of 16 who had produced for her teacher as an attempt at literature a dull, poorly written, and rather thick romantic narrative. Essentially it concerned a scantily clad teenage girl who let a youth into the bedroom of her flat via the window, he having locked himself out.

The narrative proceeded as one might expect.

This piece of work was offered as an assignment for her CSE coursework folder. I thought it unacceptable and low level but the girl's teacher seems to have had few qualms about it, if any. I could go on to cite more examples and offer more comments but I will allow the work of the 15-year-old boy mentioned at the beginning of this article to speak for itself. I offer it without any further remarks.

The boy's story

One hot day in the afternoon a lad called Tim Decided to go for a walk. So he got his shoes and hat and left the house, he walked for ages through a forest down some old country roadS over a hill and into town where by then he was feeling hungry so he decided to call at a shop a buy some food at the shop Tim brought 2 sausage rolls and a coca cola, paid the lady at the till and carried on with his walk by Now it was getting late so Tim was going to turn back when he saw his mate Richard.

alright Tim Said Richard yes said tim what are you doing all the way over here when you live in the country said Richard ow I needed a walk, I was just going back actually ow said Richard Ill walk with you then said Richard. So they started walking back on the way Richard Noticed a really Nice looking bike in a shop window wow look at that bike Tim said Richard cool lets go in and have a proper look said tim Tim and richard went in to have a good look at the bike, look at the suspension forks on it yea and the XTR Groupset I wonder how much it costs said Richard Why don't we ask said tim so Tim asked the owner how much it cost the man said well with the XTR Groupset, DH forks and a Titanium frame a long with the carbon rimed wheels you can have it for £2000 wow said Tim and richard and decideed it would be a while before they could afford anything like that and went home.   The end

✳ ✳ ✳ *BREAK ...*

More is better – or is it? – Gavin Ewart

Nobody confronted with America could say anything but
    'What a nation!'
What a genius for overdoing it, for overkill! Transport is
    'transportation',
a house is never burgled any more, it has to be 'burglarized'
and instead of being tailored things are 'customized'.
They never shorten anything – that would make it less
    important –
they inflate the English language in a way they certainly
    oughtn't
to, indeed everything goes into officialese, a kind of
    gobbledygook
invented by the sort of people who never open a
    (hardcover) book.
And they're prudish with it. A cock gets to be a 'rooster',
a bull is 'a male cow'. What a confidence-booster
to think that the Fate of the Western World, subject to every
    kind of delay, difficulty and technical hitch
is in the hands of fellows who can't bring themselves to call
    a hound a bitch!

'As of now,' 'at this moment in time' and that dream word
    'situation' –
surely such phrases as these have degenerated
    communication?
But in this ghastly patois 'meet up with' is most gooey –
in those innocent far-off days they said 'Meet me in St.
    Louis!'
and it was always 'meet me' in those old-fashioned
    conditions,
but communal self-importance has added two needless
    prepositions.
I don't so much mind 'talk with' instead of 'talk to', but no
    colloquial myth

is going to be established by saying 'I gave him a good
        talking-with'.

But most terrible of all is how stupidly and dopefully
they use (and we use) that ubiquitous 'hopefully.'
Two birds with one stone are said to be killable
but they've done the reverse – by adding an extra syllable
to the 'I hope' or 'We hope'. And without getting into
        digressions or sermons
I can tell you that *hoffentlich* is not used so much, in this
        way, even by the Germans.
It's a wounded language – with transplants, amputation,
        suture –
when we've made a nonsense of a sentence like 'He
        looked forward hopefully to the future.'

Perhaps it is more logical to say 'on the street', not 'in the
        street' –
which suggests people under manhole covers and other
        people's feet –
and another thing that I myself haven't any doubt of
is that it's neater to say 'out the window' than 'out of,'
and 'gobbledygook' itself is a wonderful word – but when
        you've said that you've said it,
that's about all that can be chalked up to America's credit.

TURNING TO NOD GOODBYE

Josephine Crilly

Cyberspeak is ubiquitous. Many cyber-words, for example,
download, laptop, and modem are euphonious, enriching the
language. They are not loanwords, but here in their own right.
Other terminologies, especially that of metrication, are cuckoos in
the nest. In turfing out the venerable words, they deprive the
language of colour and warmth.

Arnold Bennett said that all change, albeit for the better, is always accompanied by drawbacks and discomforts. One regrets the inevitable parting with words that have served us since Anglo-Saxon times and were here before King Alfred. Many arrived with William the Conqueror. Others were absorbed in Shakespeare's time, often from the great literatures of Greece and Rome. Soldiers, sailors and traders brought home idioms from distant lands.

Some words die and are forgotten, but many of those which wrapped themselves about us like comfy old coats are stolen off our backs. So we don *hectares, litres* and *milligrams* – but not, I hope, without turning to nod goodbye respectfully to the earliest form of English bequeathed by our ancestors.

> *I like that ancient Saxon phrase which calls*
> *the burial-ground Gods-Acre!*
>
> Longfellow

Only in phrases like Gods-Acre and broadacre does acre still mean a field of sorts. Correctly, an acre is a measure of 4,840 square yards of land, whereas Old English *aecer* was the field – a piece of land cleared for ploughing or grazing. An acre's precise definition varied according to time and place. A farmer was an acreman who paid a firma, or fixed rent.

Later an acre was a strip of open field, large enough to be ploughed by a yoke of oxen in one day. To help the ploughman measure his 4,840 square yards, a chain 22 yards long was laid along the field's headland, showing the width to be ploughed. From here he would plough furlongs (i.e. a furrow long), of 10 chains or 220 yards. Come Sunday, the ploughman might mark out the village cricket pitch, having borrowed the farmer's chain: 22 yards exactly.

Persons of a certain age learned by rote that eight furlongs make a mile, and since the 9th century, a furlong has described an eighth part of an English mile, regardless of its agricultural definition.

From time immemorial we have used our bodies for measuring – by foot, for example. An ell, Anglo-Saxon *eln*, was a rough reckoning, being the distance from the crook of the arm to the end of the longest finger, the elbow being where the bow or bend occurred. Bow is from an old verb, *bugan* to bend, and is at the root of rainbow, bow (tie), and bow (and arrow).

Using our fingers, we counted in tens. Numbers 11 and 12 emphasise this finger-reckoning. After ten sheep had passed him, the shepherd had used up all his fingers. Many etymologists believe that *endleofon* is the Old English form for 'left after ten, one left over.' Twelve in Old English was *twa-lif* or *twelf*, when two (more than ten) were left.

To tell meant to count (as in telling the beads of a rosary); a tale was a reckoning. In *L'Allegro*, Milton writes:

> *And every shepherd tells his tale*
> *Under the hawthorn in the dale.*

In 'telling his tale', every shepherd counted his sheep as they went past him. We still tell the time.

A *hand-span* is the stretch from thumb to little finger. According to Dr. Johnson, *span new* was the term applied to cloth immediately after taking it off the *spannans*, or stretchers.

A rod, pole, or perch was measured by a stick, the Old English *rodd* being 5½ yards. The area of an acre was standardized by Edward I as being land 40 rods long by 4 rods wide. Yard (OE *gyrd, geard*) is of superior stock: the earth itself was *middangeard*, 'middle-yard,' being the place between the abode of the gods and the abode of giants. As a suffix it survives in churchyard, dockyard, and shipyard.

Until about 1150, Old English time was reckoned by nights, not by days, for the Anglo-Saxon language flourished in lands where nights were long and the days fleeting periods of light. The light of learning, notes Simeon Potter in *Our Language*, shone more brightly in Northumbria than anywhere else in Europe. Northumbria was then on the periphery of the civilised world.

North American friends rightly regard as archaic my use of *fortnight*, this word being a survival of the old way of reckoning two weeks, by using 'fourteen-night'. Shakespeare uses *sevennights* for week when the three weird sisters chant:

> *Weary se'ennights, nine times nine*
> *Shall he dwindle, peak, and pine.*   [Macbeth]

Reckoning by nights is a relic of the Celtic custom of starting the day at sunset. In the Book of Genesis too, evening always precedes morning:

> *The evening and the morning were the first day ...*

The time between light and dark, *twilight*, is of the same root as *two, twain, twixt*, and *tween*, from Old English *twa*.

A certain drama is attached to words prefixed by *night-*. From Old English *galen*, to sing, comes nightingale, simply 'the singer by night'. Deadly nightshade, woody nightshade, the narcotic plants commonly known as belladonna and bittersweet, have their origins in Old English *nihtscad* – *niht* 'night' and *scada* 'shade'. Old English *mare* in 'nightmare' means demon or devil. Tennyson writes of 'the black bat, night', Shakespeare of 'the foul womb of night'. Better sleep might have resulted from taking a *nightcap* or grog (whisky preferred) before bedtime, helped too by wearing a *night cap*.

Small units of time – *second, minute* and *hour* – are borrowed from Latin *secundus, minuta* and *hora*. *Year, month, week* and *day* are Old English *gear, monao, wice* and *daeg*. 'Day' has poetical overtones. The daisy flower closes its pink-tipped petals (lashes), and goes to sleep when the sun sets. In the morning the petals open to the light. Anglo-Saxon for daisy was *daeges eage*, 'day's eye'.

The Bible uses *dayspring* for the beginning of the day; also for the commencement of the Messiah's reign:

The dayspring from on high hath visited us. [Luke i ,78]

Old English *springan* (German *springen*) became 'spring', but an older word for that season marks a period of the Church Year: *Lent*. The Saxons' March was *lencten*. Lenten food being frugal and stinted, Shakespeare has 'lenten entertainment' in Hamlet, a 'lenten answer' in Twelfth Night, and a 'lenten pye' in Romeo and Juliet.

Lent lily is the older name for the daffodil:

When daffodils begin to peer,
With heigh! the doxy, over the dale,
Why, then comes in the sweet o' the year,
For the red blood reigns in the winter's pale.
[A Winters Tale, IV ii, 1]

Of unknown origin, *doxy* is variously the low term for sweetheart or 'mistress, female tramp or beggar, plaything or paramour [toy boy?], even a baby'. In the West of England, babies were called doxies.

The oldest words, for example *wife, live, fight, love, sleep* and *house*, relate to home and family. They also include the counting of time and measuring of space, the meeting of communities, the working of the soil and caring for beasts.

It was not called Anglo-Saxon by those who spoke it, but 'Englisc' from *Engle* 'Angles', Anglo-Saxon being simply the earliest form of the language.

William Burroughs has said that words are an 'around-the-world, oxcart way of doing things, awkward instruments,' eventually to be laid aside. He was thinking of the space age and no doubt would have included the cyberworld. But Richard Morrison, writing in *The Times* in 1995, says he knows a journalist who has taken to writing his stories in longhand, revising them laboriously in ink, and only then tapping them into the computer. When Morrison asked why he did that, his friend answered, 'So that posterity can compare the various drafts. Shakespeare would have understood.'

LETTING IT ALL HANG OUT

Adrian Williams

'That's a hanging participle,' said Dr Slater, a note of accusation in her tone, as we loitered in the coffee-queue some fifty years ago.

She was a PhD and I was an undergraduate, so it was according to the acceptable workings of etiquette that she should thus upbraid me. It happened that our mutual academic interest was mathematics and not English, but I was intrigued nevertheless and asked her to explain.

'Having said that, the computer doesn't do fixed-point operations very well,' she quoted back at me. 'The computer did not say that. It cannot speak. It was you who said it.' She probably went on to explain that, had I begun with that said, she would not have cavilled.

The experience must have affected me deeply, since I remember the circumstances so clearly. I became an instant enthusiast for the rooting-out of hanging participles, and pursued them and hunted them down for many years. But, looking back over the years, I have come round to the view that fervour of this sort is misdirected. To be sure, it's a great thing to be able to recognise a hanging participle – but does a hanging participle matter, so long as the meaning is clear?

A truly hanging participle (or dangling or unattached participle) is one that relates to nothing in the sentence around it. Then the sentence can be difficult to understand, or it can irritate the reader. Here is a recent example from a letter to the *Oxford Times*:

> *Lying immediately adjacent to the listed St Barnabas Church, one would have thought the most appropriate approach was to echo the glories of the church in the design of the new flats.*

To what does lying apply? To understand what was being discussed, the reader needed to search in the previous paragraph, for the proposed public square. That, for me, was a search too far.

Here is the Head of Riverside Girls' High School in Sydney, quoted in *The Economist*

> *We [discuss] all the terms for white settlement: colonialism, invasion and genocide … If the prime minister wants a single narrative instead, then speaking as someone who's taught history for 42 years he'll have an absolute fight on his hands.*

I was brought up short by this statement, not realising that John Howard had been so long a history-teacher – until I perceived that the Head of Riverside was referring to herself. Perhaps if I had been in the room when she spoke to the press, I would have understood her, and would have accepted her statement without objection.

How should we regard this example from *Radio Times*?

> *Famous for his industrial landscapes and matchstalk figures, Rolf [Harris] meets people who knew the artist LS Lowry …*

The focus of my attention here, famous, is not a participle – nor indeed is it hanging, because it is attached (albeit rather remotely) to LS Lowry. But the usage had me frowning, momentarily, as I tried to conjure up the industrial landscapes that had made Rolf Harris famous.

Here is a real beauty, spotted on the label of an exhibit in Bath's Holburn Museum. Before the reader can attach the participle to its intended target, he needs to contain his impatience across 27 words (including four nouns that might have been the target), and to dive to the end of a dependent clause:

> *Already traversed just 40 years earlier by the Kennet and Avon Canal, Brunel was able to convince protesters that the railway would be a major attraction for the [municipal] gardens.*

The offence that hanging particles gives to the reader is not really the offence of being bad syntax; it is the offence of distracting the reader from his goal of understanding the meaning. Sometimes, a hanging particle can hang quite happily without distracting the reader or listener at all: assuming that you're free tomorrow, will you go to London? for example, or, talking about TV, do your friends watch Celebrity Big Brother?

So, Dr Slater, can we call it quits? I am all for clarity, and I am grateful to you for educating me in how to spot this beast in the syntactical jungle. But spotting it is one thing – castigating it is another. Hanging my participles does not have to be a hanging offence.

❊ ❊ ❊ *BREAK ...*

The Lord's Prayer

A politically correct version devised by the Reverend Kenneth Scott of Ontario

Our universal chairperson in outer space, your identity enjoys the highest rating on a prioritised selectivity scale. May your sphere of influence take on reality parameters;

may your mindset be implemented on this planet as in outer space.

Allot to us, at this point in time and on a per diem basis, a sufficient and balanced dietary food intake, and rationalise a disclaimer against our negative feed-back as we rationalise a disclaimer against the negative feedback of others.

And deprogram our negative potentialities, but desensitise the impact of the counterproductive force. For yours in the dominant sphere of influence, the ultimate capability, and the highest qualitative analysis rating, at this point in time; and extending beyond a limited time-frame.

End of message.

FROM PRIVATE GRIEF TO PUBLIC CULTURE

AG Dowell Lee

It took an unexpected stay in an Italian hospital and a realistic dramatisation of the Odyssey in a Mediterranean setting on television to start my mind on two related trains of thought. The first was of the Greek businessman, parent of one of my pupils, who as a child at his grandmother's knee had learned to recite large chunks of Homer in Classical Greek. I suspect that there was not a lot to do on a Greek island during the long winter evenings, and I have no idea how accurate his Homeric Greek is, but there really is something substantially impressive about a culture whose spoken language and ideas endure in men's minds for nearly three millennia. Oral language has a power when detached from a printed text.

For less obvious reasons, my mind returned a few years to my experiences when teaching Form J4 for most of the curriculum, including Reading. As a result of one of those perennial emergencies which are the staple of English school life, as Principal, I had to decide whether to subject J4 to an unpredictable regime of supply teachers or to step in myself. To tell the truth, after many years spent advising teachers, I rather looked forward to keeping my eye in with a mixed ability, co-educational group of 8-year-olds.

It seems to me that one of the recent weaknesses of English teaching in primary schools has been the learning of Reading. Even in good schools with the teaching mainly by phonic methods, it tends to be largely one-to-one instruction, whether it is the teacher hearing the child read in school, or the parent at home. The child progresses well until it reaches a so-called Mechanical Reading Age of about 10 years when it can decipher common printed words into spoken sounds. At this point it is deemed to be ready for library books.

From then on, nobody hears the child read out loud, assuming forlornly that the ear for literature and personal pleasure will progress hand in hand. Reading becomes a private activity (or inactivity), a private pleasure, or as often as not a private grief. Frequently, the child's reading age regresses.

Recent Inspectors' Reports and exam results indicate a real national problem, with no suggested solution apart from the inevitable panacea expenditure on computers. The J4 Experience may offer a few pointers.

The link between my two trains of thought which at first eluded me was the class reading book, *Charlotte's Web* by EB White. As a class teacher, I have always instinctively preferred the term class learning to teaching since it is the activity not the teaching which ultimately produces the learning.

At the moment of meeting J4 they had almost finished their class reader. They were sure they had. We've finished it. We need the next one. They were unanimous. Well, show me, I said. So they did. One by one, weak or confident, they struggled through, word by word, until the next one took over. They did well, decrypting the printed word into something approaching speech. To be fair, it was language; but it was not English; well, not the sort that we constantly claim as our proud legacy to world culture.

For those who have not yet met *Charlotte's Web*, it is an enthralling book, what John Buchan would have called a 'gripping yarn', ideal for 8-year-olds and me. It is the story of a Mid-western farmer's daughter who adopts Wilbur, the runt of the litter, with the happy outcome that he avoids becoming tomorrow's breakfast and survives to become the County Champion Pig. By coincidence the hired hand's name is Homer, but the fascination lies in the almost Homeric structure of the story. It is told on two levels throughout, not mortals and immortals, but humans and the most anthropomorphic animals you ever did see in barn or yard.

The centre of the plot is the Penelope-like character of Charlotte, the Spider, who weaves and re-weaves her web daily, combining a Delphic ability to spell out cryptic messages to such effect in the fabric. The vocabulary of the book is wide and the grammar challenging, but above all readable. It is worthwhile and rewarding to perfect the reading of almost every sentence. There aren't many books you could say that of.

However, listening to their efforts, it was evident that, far from having finished *Charlotte's Web*, in reality they had hardly started it. They might be able to say the right words in the right order, but they had not got near to the Meaning and the Feeling. It was not Literature. The idea that such things automatically follow the rendering of the words is pathetic illusion and responsible for much of our poor language teaching. There seems to be an almost universal belief among language teachers that language is made up of words and that words have meaning. The reality is that words have definitions to be found in dictionaries. They only acquire their full meaning when used in phrases (or in those dreaded idioms so beloved of nineteenth century textbook writers), and only then. Phonics are the beginning of reading, but Meaning and Feeling are the ends. Printed words need to be turned into Literature. This stage had not yet arrived for J4.

So we started reading again as a group activity (for my benefit you understand) with much repetition, this time making sure that every word was understood and that it was phrases rather than lone words that were said; weaker readers were helped by the stronger. Tricky bits were practised chorally as if they were tongue-twisters. Punctuation gave shape and meaning to the sentences. Vocal cadence added colour and feeling. It was hard work and slow going, but every bit worth while. I am convinced that such bridge-work is essential to close the gap between the printed page and Literature.

It is arguable that the Oral Link is the weakest element in our primary school education system. As a nation we are hung up on teaching Received Standard Pronunciation for fear of appearing to suggest that the child's family accent is common, regardless that over much of Europe children learn effortlessly to be bilingual – dialect at home and national at school. Indeed, in frontier regions, they acclimatise to one or more foreign languages as well. Only in England do we leave the problems of other languages until the age of 12-plus, with evident – and predictable – results.

The core problem of teaching reading lies in the one-to-one approach – the inevitable helper who hears them read. Any correction of pronunciation has to be personal or hesitant and may be resented by someone. By teaching reading as a group activity, a social or a choral activity, almost as if it were elocution, it ceases to be personalised and is as pleasurable as the choruses in the Messiah. From the teacher's point of view it is surprising how much detail of personal variants can be detected and corrected in a choral effort without appearing to pick on any individual.

By clearly linking the cadence of the voice to the punctuation and the meaning, the same links become available in reverse automatically. If what a child has written is read clearly with meaning, the punctuation becomes obvious. Coupled with learning verse by heart, I am convinced that this is the sort of activity by which printed Literature can enter the mind and hence be passed on to succeeding generations, eventually to become Culture.

RULES FOR WRITERS

William Safire – (submitted by Adrian Stokes)

- Remember to never split an infinitive.

- The passive voice should never be used.

- Do not put statements in the negative form.

- Verbs has to agree with their subject.

- Proofread carefully to see if you words out.

- If you reread your work, you can find on rereading a great deal of repetition can be avoided by rereading and editing.

- A writer must not shift your point of view.

- And don't start a sentence with a conjunction.

- Remember, too, a preposition is a terrible word to end a sentence with.

- Don't overuse exclamation marks!!

- Place pronouns as close as possible, especially in long sentences, as of 10 or more words, to their antecedents.

- Writing carefully, dangling participles must be avoided.

- If any word is improper at the end of a sentence, a linking verb is.

- Take the bull by the hand and avoid mixing metaphors.

- Avoid trendy locutions that sound flaky.

- Everyone should be careful to use a singular pronoun with singular nouns in their writing.

- Always pick on the correct idiom.

- The adverb always follows the verb.

- Last but not least, avoid clichés like the plague; seek viable alternatives.

THOUGHTS ON AN ENGLISH ACADEMY

Michael Gorman

The idea of an English Academy, or Institute, or Authority, will not go away. There is something there which we feel instinctively would be worth while, and this document tries to identify what that might be.

The aim of such an institute might be stated simply as to support and promote Standard English. The means by which it might do this are many.

- To advocate the case for Standard English: its benefits to individuals and its benefits to states and societies resulting from accurate and detailed exchange of information, emotion, and judgement; and from the storage of these exchanges for future readers.

- To encourage updated editions of standard works, such as the major dictionaries and other guides to grammar and style.

- To monitor the standards and results of public examinations in England and elsewhere.

- To be aware of popular concern for or indifference to language issues, and to promote public debate on these.

- To be aware of academic and industrial research into language, to review it at both professional and popular levels, and to assess present or future practical benefits of that research.

- To maintain a first-class library of books, videotapes, CDROMs, and other media covering the art of literature and the science and history of language. English in all its major varieties would be the main concern, but other languages would be held for comparative or historical reasons.

- To transcribe material from one medium to another where generally useful.

What sort of organisation do we need for this? Let us look at two sorts of organisations: the institutes associated with universities but independent of them; and the Royal Society. These bodies are respected as academically sound, and are incorporated in a legal and practical way. The activities mentioned above are of course much more than rescarch, and for example entail genuine communication with the public.

Vital to the success of such a body are the governing staff. We would need an almost saintly compound of knowledge and love of English, a sense of commitment to such an institute, academic insight, worldly-wise experience, ability to co-operate with colleagues, financial integrity, and plain old common sense. Clearly such a body is on the million pound scale financially. Can we get there in one bound? Probably not. Can we get there by beginning with some of the activities indicated above? I hope so.

These are some preliminary ideas. I suggest we need to consult within the QES, and with academics, media folk, employers, and the public to remove some of these ideas, modify others, and add further ones until we have something which can be widely supported. I hope at that stage it will still amount to something worthwhile.

✳ ✳ ✳ *BREAK ...*

The British journalist – by Fritz Spiegl

You cannot hope to bribe or twist,
Thank God! the British journalist.
But, seeing what the man will do
Unbribed, there's no occasion to.

(Humbert Wolfe, ca. 1910)

No bribes, maybe, but freebie trips
On train and planes and pleasure ships.
Books and records to review
Are flogged for cash – *merci beaucoup*.

Chateau de Plonque and *Piat d'Or*,
Arrive in van-loads at his door.
(He may not have much of a nose
But knows the wine-buff's purple prose).

The Motoring scribe is lent a car,
Dined, with champagne and caviar,
To publish what he really thinks
- but never says 'This model stinks.'

His grammar isn't very good:
While you are standing, he is stood;
And where you're sitting, he is sat –
Our youngsters cannot cope with that.

The passive or the active voice?
He doesn't know there is a choice;
And when it comes to 'whom' and 'who'
He simply hasn't got a clue.

'If I was' or 'If I were'?
Our man can see no difference there.
No Greek or Latin light his way,
He can't distinguish 'might' from 'may.'

And yet he does his level best
To treat each headline as a jest
And always tries to lend some fun
To bad news with a feeble pun:

Painter drops dead? The clever hack
Will head the story ART ATTACK!
Italian tenor dies? OK,
Bring out the headline: PASTA WAY.

His diners never eat but 'munch',
Decision-time 'comes to a crunch',
Champagne is 'sipped' and ale is 'quaffed',
Hats never taken off but 'doffed'.

Coyly changing 'days' to 'daze',
His wild mis-spellings would amaze
A teacher in an infants' school.
He never memorised a rule:

Siege or seige? I before e?
It matters not 'to I and we'.
Lie or lay or laid or lain?
He fails to make his meaning plain,

In jest he mixes poles with polls,
Gives cobblers souls and parsons soles,
Conceits that earned him and his buddies
Their BA (Hons) in Media Studies.

You cannot hope to bribe or twist,
Thank God! the British journalist?
Maybe. But oh, it makes you sick
How the old craft's gone down the nick.

REFORM WILL ONLY SPELL DISASTER

SLR Kellett

The idea of a phonetic reform of spelling is 100 years old and as silly now as it was when George Bernard Shaw proposed it. On teaching practice in Tyneside I found my pupils regularly spelt rain as *rian*, rhyming with *paean*, because that was how they pronounced the word.

If we reform our spelling, should we write rain as *reyn, rine* (or *ra-in*), *rehn, ren, rian* or *reen*? How would reformed spelling distinguish between *aw, awe, or, ore* and *oar*? Whatever we choose will fail someone. Such chaos makes it hell to read Tudor documents which were spelled phonetically at whim. Only Finnish and SerboCroat have phonetic spelling, and they suffer from dialect variants.

A written language is a visual convention read visually, and cannot be reproduced phonetics. In Romanised phonetic Japanese, *ki* means a tree, steam, spirit, power; *senko* has 16 meanings. It takes nearly 10,000 characters to be literate in Chinese or Japanese. How do their children cope? By developing visual memory, as should ours.

Functional 'illiterates' *can* read but haven't developed the skill to do so fluently by practising with a wide range of texts. A nation of TV watchers is bound to be tempted into such illiteracy.

The Chinese Communists 'simplified' their characters, allegedly for children's benefit but in reality to destroy awareness of the past. They failed and have had to backtrack. The Initial Teaching Alphabet was a similar failure here.

We should beware of any more patronising attempts to prevent our children from learning the skills every written language will always require.

ENGLISH – A LANGUAGE WORTH FIGHTING FOR

Tim Austin

It's surprising how many people cannot spell 'seize': or, to put it another way, its suprising that peoples' inability to spell 'sieze' are so widespread.

Now, how many elementary spelling/grammatical mistakes can you spot in the second part of that sentence? If you find more than five, do let me know.

Perhaps you think it doesn't matter that *its* (the possessive of it), and *it's* (abbreviation of 'it is', have different meanings) or that the possessive of people (a plural noun) is people's (except in rare cases such as when you write, say, of the peoples of Africa): but many of us do still think such distinctions are important, indeed vital, to protect some formality and purity in the English language.

Moreover, your insouciance about such things could cost you dearly. If your job application is riddled with spelling mistakes and grammatical errors, many prospective employers will reject you out of hand. My job as chief revise editor of *The Times* entails scouring the paper for all kinds of errors – factual as well as spelling, grammar and tone – so I come into daily contact with the commonest solecisms and lapses of linguistic concentration that collectively would undermine the paper's authority.

Yes, *Times* journalists – often writing and subediting at breakneck speed to meet deadlines – do sometimes slip up, and when they do, we have an army of hawk-eyed readers ready to pounce on our sins and omissions and tell us in no uncertain terms.

They are quite right to do so, too. Responsible media such as *The Times* and the BBC have a duty to maintain high standards in the use of English: not to preserve it in aspic, but to let it evolve as a vital, organic language in a reasoned and orderly way.

We all lapse into the vernacular when we speak, understandably so. We all say 'none were' rather than 'none was' or 'neither good or bad' rather than 'neither good nor bad'. Speaking, however, is not the same as writing. When we write, we should try harder. Too many writers disconnect their participles. 'Driving over the hill, the sun shone brightly on the valley ahead' is nonsense: the sun is not doing the driving. Singulars and plurals are too often mixed in the same sentence. Such examples devalue our rich and subtle language. They are lazy and thoughtless. We should also try to avoid clichés such as *bombshell, escalate* or *unique*.

Grammar, particularly, seems to be a generational problem. Some of our journalists in their twenties and thirties, though talented and bursting with enthusiasm, ideas and knowledge, are from the generation never taught formal grammar at school. Occasionally they need old fogeys like me to keep them on the grammatical straight and narrow.

But the generation game works both ways. I and colleagues in their forties, fifties and above, have to be ready to adapt to new terminology, not to become encrusted in a mould of linguistic inflexibility.

Language is important. It can help you to find a job; used properly, but not pedantically, it can give your image a boost; it can give you self-confidence. But you need to think about, it, to work at it and not to give in to its easy temptations. Seize the opportunity and you may be surprised how much you enjoy it.

✳ ✳ ✳ *BREAK ...*

Twas Brillig ... Janice Booth

We've mortgages rising by half a per cent,
So homes are cheap neither in Sussex or Kent.
'Deceptively spacious' means nothing at all -
Quite small but looks large? Or immense but looks small?
If Maximus hadn't been killed by a spear
Then he may have survived and be presently here.
Now fasten your belt and remain in your seat
For the plane's momentarily landing in Crete.
Its hard for a horse which is casting it's shoe;
Such prose begs the question – just whose teaching who?
Between you and I, having started to write it,
This rhyme's getting worse – but I'll press on despite it.
A childrens' emporium, certain to please,
Stocks 100's of ice's and colour TV's.
Its bound to contain a percentage of toy's,
Comprising of things for both girl's and for boys'.
Oh pity the teacher who's subject is grammar
She'll either develop a squint or a stammer.
Not only does usage cause venom and rages
But also discussions that drag on for ages.
I'm certain the English above isn't your's
So lets have a mutual round of applause!

NOTES FROM AN EDITOR'S DESK

James Alexander

It is always immensely cheering to read letters and other
contributions in the magazine which point out some amazing mis-
uses of English. It is reassuring to find that other people are just as
incensed as I am about the degeneration of our extraordinary
language. Debates rage on about the most obvious annoyances

such as split infinitives and aberrant apostrophes, but there are other frequently found problems in books, newspapers, on shop signs and in virtually every form of printed material. As editor to a wide range of writers with differing understandings of grammar and English in general, I find that occasionally I have to laugh out loud when some particular howler leaps off the page at me. This is not to say that I take unfair and malicious amusement from my writers, but they would be the first to acknowledge that they need editorial services.

With a few minor changes to preserve copyright, I would like to share some of the problems with you. A common dilemma for writers is whether or not to include commas. This indecision has caused me headaches on several occasions. For example, 'he exhibited the device which he had built out of parts from a scrap heap on the manager's desk.' 'The men who were left behind had to wait for the turning of the tide.' This latter example is more devious – how many men were left behind – all of them or just some? In the context, the example shown is correct, although the original had two commas, one after 'men' and one after 'behind'. Or this: 'The dog growled and ran up to the woman tugging at her raincoat.' Who, one asks, was the one doing the tugging? Many of my clients would readily confess to being confused by punctuation. Some exhibit a reckless abandon, sprinkling dots and dashes, commas and quote marks ad lib, others seem frightened to put any at all. It is surprising what difference a minute little squiggle of ink can make to the sense of a sentence. 'Running over his friend Richard Jones laughed out loud.' This gives at least three comma-placing variations. And how about '... they stood still lost in each other's arms'? Which side of the 'still' should I place the comma?

Similar problems occur with hyphens. Try the sense of these: 'Care should be taken with drinking water at sea.' 'He stormed into his world shattering illusions.' 'We decided to buy a second hand cart for the farm.' 'SOCO found a clear cut finger print.' In fact, the sense of these sentences demanded three hyphens and one comma – drinking-water, second-hand and clear-cut, but not world-shattering, where a comma was needed. A clearer construct would have been, 'Shattering illusions, he stormed into his world.'

Although not necessarily of the writer's making, sometimes a typo creates a problem. Recently, I found 'No tall people will be admitted,' rather than 'not all ...' And, of course, the ridiculously simple-minded spell-checker would accept the first version without demur. As it did when a secretary sent a letter which resulted in the recipient bawling out the sender over the telephone, saying, 'How dare you be so patronising!' The secretary had ended the letter, 'I hope to see you son.' 'Soon' would have been better!

It seems to me that many writers do not read their own script carefully before submission. Either that, or they cannot recognise errors which they themselves have made (I realise that I am opening myself to criticism here, expecting this text to be perfect!). The following sentences have appeared before me: 'The maximum penalty for killing someone with a car is five years.' Do you receive a harsher sentence for killing someone who only owns horses? (Does this question refer to a person who owns nothing other than horses? - should it be 'owns only horses'? and so on ...) Two real gems must have escaped the writer's checking procedure when she wrote, 'The weather halved our attendance by half.' And, even more curious mathematically, 'If we do not take care, the project will repercuss back on us again.' By my reckoning, that is sheer overkill – to repercuss, to do it back and then do it back again!

Silly faults in written English can cause amusement but they do have the effect of making the reader stop and retrace steps to find the actual meaning of the sentence. It rarely happens in conversation or in any form of public speaking. The simple expedient of re-reading one's own writing should show up such errors. I know that I am kidding myself by saying things like that. There are very few people who find even the most basic and simple error obvious. This is surely the fault of the education system but also of a slap-happy, it-doesn't-really-matter attitude to language that is insidiously creeping into modern life.

These sentences are not good, but how many people would halt and question the constructions – if, indeed, they noticed a problem in the first place? 'Why am I attracted to partners I would rather not people I respect see me with?' 'The firm was teetering on the brink of imminent bankruptcy.' (Tautologies are amongst the most difficult of written errors to pick up, as they usually sound so plausible and correctly emphatic, as in '... but until a significant consensus of opinion is of a similar mind, nothing will change.') 'Customers please refrain from entering the workshops due to new safety laws.' ' Unwarranted slaughter would wipe out half our herd which it has taken a lifetime to build up.' Why the 'it'?

I can add a pretty sign to the apostrophe debate – seen outside a shop in Maidenhead was a well produced and colourful notice saying – Xma's tree's. It was obviously believed to be correct as there was another sign just like it a few yards farther on. And what of the notice in a branch of Tesco which stated – 'Customers wanting their bread slicing should ask at the counter'. 'Sliced' would be correct. Such nonsenses are legion and yet so many people do not even notice, or, what is worse, see these signs and think them to be correct, then use the same constructs themselves. Children cannot expect to become adequate spellers and grammarians when words such as 'tonite', 'kwik' or 'shoos' are used regularly by shops and other commercial enterprises. A sign seen recently in a reputable store showed C.D''s – yes one stop and two apostrophes. Quite a few rogue apostrophes (Sauterne's and bargain's amongst others) were also spotted recently in two French wine stores, claiming to attract the English bargain hunter. Where will it end?

To return to the editor's desk for a moment, another serious problem for many writers is the choice offered by a range of homophones, when the right word is not ingrained on the mind. Many writers confuse 'whose' and 'who's'; 'too', and 'to'; 'where' and 'we're'; 'their', 'there' and 'they're'; and of course the perennial 'its' versus 'it's'. One learned management book I was editing had presented so many 'it's' - or should that be 'it'ses' (or it's's)? - by chapter two that I used the 'change all' command on the computer and it found 135 other examples in the book. It was easier to correct the occasional 'its' back to 'it's' when needed, than go through all the wrong 'it is' errors which actually should have been 'belonging to it'. I hope it's clear. Less obvious homophones we have recently found include 'doe' for 'dough', 'site' for 'cite' and 'soul' for 'sole', and examples such as 'it was a might too close' and 'residents of warmer climbs'.

Changes in plurality, which seem to be more common these days – and, I am sorry to say, more acceptable – stand out from the page like blisters. Why do so many people find this ugliness so unexceptional? 'Every patient may see their records.' Ugh! 'None of these arguments apply, do they?' Ugh! 'None of us are identical.' Awful! Even illustrious chief editors of national dailies now condone these plural shifts.

Perhaps I had an exceptional English teacher who was able to appeal to my sense of correctness and logic and ingrain these basic grammatical patterns into my young mind. The poor old fellow succumbed to Parkinson's eventually, but he clearly made his mark with me before going to the great grammaticum in the sky. It has been a lifetime's interest and I do not think that I am alone. However, the few of us left need to stand up for the correct use of our excellent and most versatile language in the face of all opposition from the lazy, the uninterested, the casual and the careless. It does matter. Taking the easy option and dumbing down reduce the brilliance of English, which must be a constantly evolving and improving language, not a shrinking and ragged apology for a language.

Clearly there are occasions when a linguistic lapse is acceptable – even necessary – to make a point or to report speech correctly. But the neatness and acceptability of written English does still depend so very much on its being done correctly. 'Hear hear!' do I hear you say (not 'here here!' as one recent writer had it!). Then go forth and preach, my friends.

ALL THINGS CONSIDERED

Colin M Johnson

This morning I met a neighbour who asked me: 'How are things?'

I began by telling him that many of them aren't what they used to be, whereupon he gave me a funny look and hurried away. That's what you get these days for being pedantic.

I wanted to tell him that up in our attic we have a vast collection of things, the accumulated clutter of half a century, including the occasional thing of the past. I cannot claim we have all kinds of things up there – we lack, for instance, a stuffed crocodile, seats from an old London taxi, a genuine Edwardian pillar box. Nevertheless, we do have an extensive variety of things like old electric drills, TV sets, and vacuum cleaners, all of which are broken or in need of repair.

My wife and I were therefore pleased to hear encouraging news from a weather man who forecast that things everywhere would improve overnight. The following morning I duly ventured into the attic, eager to check on progress, but sadly I found nothing had improved at all. Nor had any of the things which lie rusting in the garden shed. It just shows that you can't always rely on weather men.

Mind you, were not like the average hoarder of things. Some years ago, the Monty Python team performed a memorable sketch about the Society for Placing Things on Top of Other Things. In our attic, however, the situation is entirely reversed. Instead of placing things one on top of the other, we actually keep most of ours hidden underneath. Maybe this is why our particular things tend to remain unaffected by wild promises from the Meteorological Office.

Still, from time to time when I've little else to do, I go up into the attic and consider all the things that we might eventually repair or dispose of. Then I come down again, having decided they can stay there till next Christmas and the New Year, or alternatively a national strike, after which some eloquent newsreader is bound to assure us yet again that things are finally getting back to normal.

SOME THOUGHTS ON STYLE

Read over your compositions and when you meet a passage which you think is particularly fine, strike it out.

Samuel Johnson

Whenever you feel an impulse to perpetrate a piece of exceptionally fine writing, obey it ... and delete it.

Sir Arthur Quiller-Couch (Q)

There is but one art, to omit.   Robert Louis Stevenson

If you wish to make an immediate improvement in your writing, cut out the word 'and' except where it joins the last two items of a list of three or more.

Le mot juste. *Whatever one wishes to say, there is one noun only by which to express it, one verb only to give it life, one adjective only which will describe it. One must search until one has discovered them, this noun, this verb, this adjective, and never rest content with approximations, never resort to trickery, however happy, or to vulgarisms, in order to dodge the difficulty.*   Guy de Maupassant

The mania for phrases. I am going on very slowly. I give myself an accursed lot of trouble. I have just suppressed phrases at the end of five or six pages, which have cost me the work of entire days. It is impossible for me to see the effect of any one of them before it is finished, re-finished and polished. It is an insane way of writing, but what can I do? I have a conviction that the things best in themselves are those that I cut out. One only succeeds in producing an effect by the negation of exuberance; but exuberance is precisely what charms me. Gustave Flaubert

. . . that accurst autobiographic form which puts a premium on the loose, the improvised, the cheap, and the easy. Save in the fantastic and the romantic it has no authority, no persuasive or convincing force – its grasp of reality and truth isn't strong and disinterested. Henry James

Since it often happens that the most obvious phrases, and those which are used in ordinary conversation, become too familiar to the ear, and contract a kind of meanness by passing through the mouths of the vulgar, a poet should take particular care to guard himself against idiomatic ways of speaking. Joseph Addison

HIGHLAND HANSARD

O Thou! Whatever title suit thee –
First Minister, or Baird, or Henry –
Fair fa' your honest Jocky face,
great chieftain o' the tartan race.
Thy speeches to the Scottish Assembly
are makin' Sassenach pedants trembly.

As we report today, Henry Baird McLeish, First Minister of the Scottish Assembly, is giving the Hansard reporters both grief and creative opportunity. His struggles with the English tongue make George W Bush sound like Cicero. His dicta are called McClichés by the bad boys and girls in his assembly. 'There is that old dictat the old ones are best' has to be amended for the record to 'dictum'. What Sam Goldwyn was to Hollywood, Henry McLeish is to Holyrood.

No parliamentary orator is a hero to his shorthand reporter. As valets tidy up the outer man, Hansard corrects and rewrites his speeches. An accurate report of anything that has ever been said in any parliament would be blather, solecism, verbiage and nonsense. Oratory was more eloquent before 1803, when Thomas Curson Hansard introduced the first allegedly reliable reports of debates. Before that Sam Johnson and other professionals were employed to impose artistic verisimilitude upon otherwise bald and unconvincing narrative. Charles Dickens reported better speeches than any contemporary MP ever made. Even today sanitised Hansard bears only an accidental identity with what is said on the floor of the House.

Matters are more complicated in the Scottish Assembly, where speech is officially allowed in three languages, English, Lallans (literary Lowland Anglo-Saxon), and Gaelic. In addition there are numerous dialects, so that a speaker in natural West Coast Scottish is immediately distinct, despised and possibly unintelligible to the posher talkers of Morningside. Doric is the dialect spoken around Aberdeen. The Official Report records an SNP member asking: 'Fit is so wrang wi wantin to speir aboot fit wye we speak at hame? I cannae see oniethin wrang wi that.'

And nor can the rest of us. Scottish is richer and more colourful than the cut-glass vowels of Received English. Burns could write memorably in both tributaries of the English tongue. Lorimer, in his translation of the New Testament into Scottish, used dozens of different dialects for the different characters. He thought about making Satan the only character to speak the Queen's English. But pawky prudence prevailed. Alas.

Hansard is history's ear, already listening. In Scotland it hears the most creative English being spoken in the kingdoms.

❋ ❋ ❋ *BREAK ...*

'Mind how you shake the ketchup bot'le,
First none'll come and then a lo'll.'   (trad.)

The letter T, it seems, is gone.
Its absence makes me boggle.
The glottal stop is all the rage,
Or should that be the glo'al?
We now put bu'er on our bread,
Our beer comes in a bo'le,
And when we want to get there fast
Just open up the thro'le.
And blame the pu'er nowadays
Each time you miss a si'er
While walking round those eighteen holes
In hope of ge'ing fi'er.
We mu'er to ourselves at times,
And moan about the clu'er,
But never think to clear it up:
Just throw it in the gu'er.
One li'le thing we all enjoy
When in our chair we se'le
Is that nice steaming cup of tea;
I hope you boiled the ke'le.
A pint of bi'er goes down well,
And when we get a le'er,
If Ernie's sent you 50 quid
Then life seems that much be'er.
But, sad to say, the T has gone;
I wonder now just wha'll
We do to try and get it back
From that awful stop that's glo'al.

LAMENT TO
THE LETTER

NOW SAY HI TO THE '

A MISSPELT YOUTH

Standards are still on the slide despite daily lessons in literacy – Laura Clark

The ability of children to spell has declined, despite a concerted Government drive to raise standards in the three Rs. An analysis of national tests has revealed that pupils aged 11 and 14 made more spelling errors last year than they did in 2000, four years into a scheme to ensure primary pupils have daily literacy lessons.

More than half of 11-year-olds struggled with common words such as *future* and *perfectly* when presented with 20 words as part of a spelling exam. Some tripped up on words such as *change* and *known*, which were often spelled *chang* and *nown* according to a report from the Government's exams watchdog. And the word *technique* stumped the vast majority of the 600,000 pupils who sat the test, with alternatives such as *techneck*, *tec-nique* and even *teacneak* given by many candidates.

Meanwhile, an analysis of spelling in the writing part of the test – which required pupils to compose a short story, scene from a play or report – showed how pupils who achieved the overall standard expected for their age spelled nine per cent of words incorrectly.

This compares with five per cent in 2000, the Qualifications and Curriculum Authority reported.

Among 14-year-olds some 5.3 errors were made per 100 words, compared with 3.9 in 2000. 'An explanation for this increase in spelling errors may be sought in the words attempted by pupils, but there was no indication that the pupils' range of vocabulary improved compared to last year. Word counts recorded similar numbers of words used and fewer scripts were judged to be in the top category for vocabulary range.' Most errors arose because pupils missed out letters, put the incorrect endings on words or used the wrong vowels.

Among seven-year-olds, spelling results improved slightly even though heads complained that the 2001 spelling test was too tough.

The slip in spelling standards among 11-and 14-year-olds emerged after researchers found a decline in primary children's ability to use simple punctuation correctly, such as capital letters and full stops.

Four years ago, Labour introduced the daily literacy hour in which teachers are responsible for ensuring that pupils can spell accurately. In summer 2000 former Education Secretary David Blunkett sent schools a list of 600 words all children should know by the end of their first year at secondary school, and the following year a list of 700 words was issued that pupils should have mastered by 14. They include *accommodation, embarrass, environment, onomatopoeia, ostinato* and *quadriceps.*

New-style English lessons introduced in secondary schools last term advise teachers to begin lessons with a ten-minute starter exercise such as spelling. Every department is expected to play a role, with maths teachers meant to drill pupils in *symmetrical* and *perpendicular*, and games teachers ensuring pupils can spell *athlete* and *quadriceps.*

The Worst Ten

techneck/tecnique   nastyest   indevidual   suprise
attemptes   themselvs   regardles   injered   desined
advetise

THE SEMI-ILLITERATES

Bill Penn

Media studies graduates don't know much about anything – least of all the media

I take a firm grip on the desk, for at any moment I may need to thrash my head several times against its surface. That's because it is graduate recruitment time again. Running a small public-relations and marketing consultancy has its rewards. It's not awfully taxing, allows me to spend a reasonable proportion of my time doing work I enjoy, and is rather profitable. No complaints there.

But one price I do pay for this life of benign contentment is that from time to time I am forced to recruit new graduates as trainees. And that's when I start thinking that really I would prefer to be cleaning the urinals at Waterloo station.

Perhaps my difficulties stem from the fact that I am not deceitful enough to employ people who are clearly too bright for a career in PR, an industry that is packed with second-raters and always has been. There are many more stimulating and useful occupations for the seriously clever.

No, what I'm after are graduates of the breeze-block universities with their degrees in marketing, communications, public relations and, yes, media studies. Of course, the latter two are the *créme de la créme*. My little heart always skips a beat when I receive a CV from a graduate of Bournemouth University, which positively teems with PR wannabes.

But then I am very discerning. Until a few years ago I took the view that people whose CVs and covering letters contained very serious grammatical and spelling mistakes were not worth interviewing. However, I ended up with so few potential interviewees that I abandoned this approach. These days I cheerfully turn a blind eye to quite grotesque errors and abuses of the English language in the search for suitable candidates.

Take this one from a young lady who wrote to us last year. Her CV detailed her various holiday jobs, including a spell as a waitress in a Knightsbridge wine bar, or, as she described it, 'a busy London brassiere'. Another defined her role with a women's theatre group as its 'pubic rations officer'. Some weeks later we heard from a marketing graduate, who provided in his application no fewer than three different spellings of his own surname, and two of his university town. Rather exotic, I thought. Childish spelling mistakes are very common. Why, only last month we had an application with no fewer than 16 in a single-page letter and short CV (graduate with a 2:1 in Marketing). Almost all such errors would be highlighted by any computer spellchecker, which I always assume these graduates are able to operate but either forget to do so or cannot be bothered. Or perhaps they have such confidence in their ability to spell that they feel they don't need any help. (This may be a good moment to point out to any media graduate reading this that liaise is not spelt L-I-A-S-E. Useful tip, eh?) Still, it's important not to be put off by these little lapses of concentration. If the covering letter is reasonably written and the CV stands up to my less than exacting standards, then an applicant bearing a media-type degree has a decent chance of being called for an interview.

That's when the fun really starts.

I have learnt not to expect too much from media studies graduates. For example, it is clearly unreasonable to assume that they will have found out anything about our company in advance of the interview. We have a website, the address of which is on our headed paper. But never mind: most of them arrive for the interview with no prior knowledge of their prospective employer. Didn't have time to look at the site, they say. Sorry.

Slightly more worrying is the fact that quite a few turn up with no idea of what public relations involves either, though they passionately declare it to be their chosen career. So, not infrequently, I interview people who know nothing about my company or what we do or what they, apparently, want to do for a living. This threatens to make the conversation with the interviewee a bit one-way, so thank goodness we have one obvious shared interest which we can discuss: the media. We deal with the media on a daily basis; they have spent three years studying it. Bingo.

But no. It seems that quite a lot of media studies graduates manage to emerge from their courses with remarkably little knowledge of, well, the media. One man (with a 2:1 class degree in the subject) had no idea what the initials BBC stand for. Nor did he know how the corporation is funded. Another couldn't quite place that chap Rupert Murdoch (he had heard of him, mind); in fact, he was unable to name a single media proprietor, past or present, not even that nasty fat man who fell off his boat a while back.

Many people I interview have never listened to Radio Four's Today programme; they tend to prefer breakfast telly. And I would say that a very high proportion simply do not read broadsheet newspapers. *The Daily Mail* seems to be the hot favourite among media graduates, but they may not look at it every day, you understand. Bit heavy-going.

Most seem unwilling to engage in any serious debate about censorship, the relationship between government and the media, privacy, or any other related issue. The problem is not so much a lack of knowledge as a serious lack of interest. I wonder how anyone can study the media for three years and yet emerge so uninvolved and uninformed. Sometimes I am moved to ask my interviewees this question directly. Usually they respond with a shrug and a snigger.

Still, there are always the film studies graduates to cheer you up. I used to imagine that I could safely indulge my mild interest in cinema with them while I decided whether they had what little it takes to succeed in public relations. Of course, I myself have very limited knowledge of the film industry, so I am always ready to bow to these graduates' superior understanding.

However, that usually turns out to be unnecessary. I am obviously out of touch with what you might expect such people to know about their subject. Recently, I interviewed two film studies graduates in the same week, neither of whom had come across such obscure figures as David Lean and Federico Fellini. I did think about calling the universities where these applicants claimed to have earned their degrees, just to check that there had not been some dreadful mistake. But then who would go to the trouble of fabricating a 2:2 in film studies?

Instead of doing this, I generally take a firm grip on the desk, picture myself, mop in hand, at Waterloo station and start thrashing.

Ah, that's better.

✸ ✸ ✸ BREAK ...

The Times ran a series of letters in which a misheard word or phrase causes amusement. They have been given the sobriquet 'Mondegreen', from the original, 'They ha' slain the Earl o' Moray and Lady Mondegreen.' (Actually '... laid him on the green').

A hymn line: 'Gladly my cross-eyed bear' (... my cross I'd bear.)

A folk dance: 'American Seat' (A Merry Conceit – can you tell the difference?)

From a Scottish friend: 'I have the Countess of Ayr to tea tomorrow ...' (the County Surveyor)

A pet-shop ad.' ..a box of puppies.' (boxer puppies)

In a letter addressed to Mr J Nasher: 'Dear Mr Nasher...' (Jane Asher, SW3)

A letter to James Hay, Solicitor, of Aberdeen: 'James Hay, Solicitor and not a republic.' (Notary Public)

A civil servant had been invited to attend a 'haddock-stirring meeting' (ad hoc steering)

A vicar's wife received a letter addressed to 'Heathfield Wreck Tree'

An ad for a child minder: '... requires help for three awful hours a week' (three or four) (They were nevertheless overwhelmed with replies!)

The MP for the Isle of Wight had a pager message: 'Good luck, please call, I love you, White Radio.'

Teletext subtitle, appearing as 'poet, SAS and critic ...' (essayist)

Directory enquiries, being asked for the number of the Wig and Pen Club, reported 'Sorry, there's no Pen Club in Wigan.'

The correspondent's wife, as a young secretary, typed '... the Church Lads' Brigade are a crazy military organisation', (quasi)

Having given his name over the phone, the writer later received a letter to 'Miss Hazel Hurst'. This prompted the use of deeper tone in future phone conversations. (Richard Hazelhurst)

On giving registration details at the start of WWII, the

correspondent's father noted that his occupation had been recorded as 'farm assistant': he had in fact said that he was a pharmacist.

A travelling comedy magician found himself with a rather different audience one night. Afterwards he found that the Birmingham Evening Mail had billed him as 'Rogers Choir'. (Roger Squires)

Finally, one from *The Times* itself: they had described the discovery, in a cave near the Dead Sea, of some 'ancient squirrels'.

… and the editor's all-time favourite – '… he was so very honoured to receive the pullet surprise.'

YOU CALLING MY EGG RACIST?

Philip Howard

'Nitty-gritty' and 'good egg' are apparently offensive terms. Nonsense!

Scene: the Police Federation conference, Bournemouth. John Denham, Home Office Minister, is speaking: 'To get down to the nitty-gritty …'

Chris Jefford, Metropolitan Police constable, interrupts him from the floor: 'That phrase is banned. If I used it, I would face a discipline charge.'

The police apparently believe that 'nitty-gritty' refers to the debris left at the bottom of a slave ship after a voyage. That is, pullulating mounds of lice and eggs of lice. That is deemed to be offensive to the descendants of slaves. To which the only possible reply is: 'Pull the other one, Flatfoot: it's got lice on.'

This is not just politically correct nonsense. It is politically moronic nonsense with stilts on. Mastery of the English language may not be the most important qualification for our police force. Few policemen, apart from fictional ones such as Adam Dalgleish and Roderick Alleyn, have been much good at English. But somebody in Scotland Yard must have access to a good dictionary. Westminster Library is just across the street.

Let us try to help them, if anybody there reads the papers. 'Nitty-gritty' is one of a huge number of rhyming jingles that occur particularly in English and other Germanic languages. They proliferate in our oldest literature such as Chaucer and Piers Plowman. Linguists call them *reduplicative* words, and the propensity of English to create them *reduplication*. Others call them *ricochet words* or *Siamese-twin words*. Scholars categorise them into groups such as onomatopoeic (bow-wow), contrived (Handy-Andy), intentional (gruesome twosome), and accidental (picnic). The first appearance of *nitty-gritty* in print was in *Time* magazine in August 1963: 'The Negroes present would know perfectly well that the nitty-gritty of a situation is the essentials of it.'

It bubbled to the surface in the States in the Sixties as part of the new groovyspeak, such as 'right-on'. Cautious lexicographers describe its etymology as 'unknown'. Less cautious ones opine: 'US Negro origin. Semantics obscure, but probably referring to unpleasant (gritty) but basic realities.' In reduplicatives, one half is the semantic driver, the other half is the jingle-jangler. Stuart Flexner in *I Hear America Singing* (Princeton, 1976) attributes the phrase to the black militants of the 1960s, and the prevalence of 'grit-like nits'.

The origin of slang, like the origin of nits, is seldom capable of proof. But new slang passes by word of mouth for only a very short period before somebody writes it down or otherwise records it.

It is inconceivable that the phrase 'nitty-gritty' lay dormant in Black American for a century after the last slave ship sailed without somebody like Harriet Beecher Stowe writing it down. If you insist on an origin, the best bet is that the gritty is the leading half of the reduplication, and the nitty is the jingle. The phrase had a great vogue in American and among those in British business and managerial circles who were keen to appear right-on and groovy. It became a thundering cliché. And died of shame. It is now very *vieux jeu* and used only jocularly.

To assert that 'nitty-gritty' is racist is as moronic as saying that 'niggardly' is an insult to black people. It is namby-pamby, niminy-piminy, airy-fairy mumbo-jumbo.

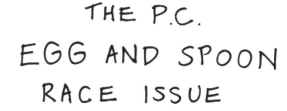

THE P.C.
EGG AND SPOON
RACE ISSUE

IT'S GOOD IN PARTS

As for the police ban on the phrase 'good egg', because of its supposed rhyming slang association with *egg and spoon/coon*, words fail us. The murderer of Macduff's son in Macbeth cries: 'What, you egg! Young fry of treachery!' Bishops and curates were fussing about bad eggs being good in parts a century ago. *Good egg* became popular slang at Oxford University while PG Wodehouse was up there. Hence the proliferation of good eggs, beans and crumpets in the Master's work.

We cannot allow the English language to be kidnapped by ignoramuses in the race relations industry or wimps among Chief Police Officer Plods. Of course, it behoves us all, including the police, to use sensitive language and not to cause offence.

The Behove is a very rare beast. Some say it is a mythical creature. The fault, dear police constable, lies not in our vocabulary, but in our canteen culture.

 **BREAK ...**

Many a mickle makes a muckle

English they say is the language most used
Most written, most spoken, most cruelly abused:

The plural of box, we all know is boxes,
Yet the plural of ox is oxen not oxes.
A goose is a goose, and two are called geese,
So why isn't more than one moose said as meese?

A mouse and his family are mentioned as mice,
But the plural of house is just houses, not hice.
The plural of brother is brothers or brethren,
And yet we say mothers, but never say methren.

The plural of man? The answer is men;
The plural of pan – who dares to say pen?
For more than one tooth we designate teeth,
Then why isn't more than one booth known as beeth?

The cow in the plural can sometimes be kine,
But who ever spoke of two vows as a vine?
You can readily double a foot and have feet;
But try as one might, you can't make root reet.

If this hand were two, then this would be these,
And yet is the plural of kiss ever kese?
We specify pronouns as he, his and him;
But never, I promise, as she, shis and shim.

No wonder that foreigners often go mad
And speak our good English atrociously bad!

SPELLING IS THE ARCHAEOLOGY OF LANGUAGE

Philip Howard

Inglish is a strange language but we should be wary of rashonalising our spelling

Its a pitty that Shakspier, who had jeneyus, was so unedicated. He's the wust speller I no ov. Down with Skool.

The latest attempt to modernise and rationalise English spelling is being launched on the Internet. It is called Freespeling. Its launcher is Richard Wade. His argument is that in our new world of mobile phones, e-mails and text messaging, we are experiencing a psychological change for technological reasons. Mobiles have very small buttons. It is slow and fiddly to write with them. Redundant letters are a nuisance in a word that you are tapping onto a mobile phone. He wants us to free spell in the way that Shakespeare did before spelling got set in concrete by dictionaries, dominies and the dreaded spell-check. We accept accents different from our own without difficulty. We even accept odd grammar like 'Don't we, innit?' But if you spell a word wrong you are regarded as ignorant or stupid. Mr Wade wants to break down the stigma to what is considered bad spelling. Why do we have to spell words such as f-u-c-h-s-i-a or y-a-c-h-t like that in the 21st century? So Mr Wade is launching a global referendum on the Internet to find every month 15 words that deserve better spelling.

His call for reform of English spelling is not new. It was expressed during the Second World War by a Dutchman whose knowledge of English was extensive and witty. His prolonged mockery of English pronunciation was published in London in the newspaper *Vrij Nederland*, the temporary organ of the Free Netherlands community in exile. After 12 stanzas comparing and contrasting the spelling of worm and storm, Job and job, and so on, his diatribe ends: 'Finally, what rhymes with tough/ though, through, plough or cough? Enough!/ Hiccough has the sound of cup/ My advice is – Give it up! '

The urge to reform the notorious difficulty of English spelling is bold as well as old. It is logical. It would be welcomed by everyone from Molesworth to students of English as a second language. It is radical and modern. And it is wrong-headed.

For English spelling is the archaeology of our old and complex language. The words stick out from the page like menhirs left there by Asterix and thousands of other invaders. Take Mr Wade's example of *yacht*. That little word contains a long and fascinating history. That ch- sound in the middle shouts Dutch. The origin of yacht is the Dutch *jacht*, short for *jaghtschip*, a ship for chasing. The present pronunciation is shown by the 17th-century spelling *yott*. A former pronunciation is shown by the spelling *yatch*, 17th to 19th century. Similarly, it would be a pity to lose the orthographic memorial to Leonhard Fuchs (1501-66). He was

Professor at Tubingen University and a pioneer of German botany. He wrote *Historia Stirpium*. The genus Fuchsia was named after him by Charles Plumier, the French botanist. The roots of the frilly seaside hedge plant are declared by its spelling.

Some of our words came into English from Latin before Hengist and Horsa arrived as early package tourists from the mainland. So our words *wine* (Latin vinum), *wall* (vallum), and *pillow* (pulvinus) show that the Latin **v**, at the time when the words were adopted into Anglo-Saxon, was pronounced more like the Anglo-Saxon **w** than any other Anglo-Saxon sound existing at the time. But pronunciations change. So do spellings. Once the English had arrived in England, they invented the letter F. Later borrowings from Latin show the later pronunciation. Hence our *fan* from Latin *vannus,* and *fiddle* from vulgar Latin *vitula*.

O kum on purleese, Filip. We cannot spell the English language for the antiquarian pleasure of pedants. Like the Tory party, we must modernise or die. Well, up to a point Lawd Koppa. You underestimate the evils of root and branch change. Whose pronunciation of English shall our spelling follow? There are more people pronouncing English in American or Indian ways than in the diverse pronunciations of the United Kingdom. Changing our spelling would cut us off from our literature as well as our etymology. Shakespeare, Jane Austen and Roald Dahl would have to be reprinted in your new spelling. Libraries would become impenetrable jungles.

English words are a mighty army, grouped into brigades, regiments and little platoons. Free spelling would reduce them to a promiscuous and barbarous horde. The English way is not revolution but evolution. Our spelling does gradually change to reflect new styles and pronunciations. It is changing in the great pond of the Internet, and the little puddles of text msging. But free-for-all spelling would deface and barbarise the English tongue. It would empty it of the hoarded wit, wisdom, poetry and history which it contains. And it ain't going to happen.

MORE ON SPELLING

Malcolm Skeggs

1,000 people were asked to find the spelling errors in the passage below. Only two got it right … and both of them were from Africa.

> *I was·borne in Yorkshire but we moved home when I was eght. I use to quarrell with my twin brother although I wasn't suppose to. Our parents were realy worried so they seperated us and sent us to diffirent schools. We were quite happy about that because we enjoyed being a part and we had plenty to tell each other during the hollidays. My brother wanted to study medecine but I prefered to study litterature. It meant I could spend my time reading books and thinking about all the wonderful caracters in them.*

Alarming evidence of a decline in educational standards emerged in a nationwide survey of spelling skills yesterday.

In one test, only two out of 1,000 people aged between 15 and 50 could pick out all 14 glaring errors in a short passage of text. Both were aged over 40 – and one came from South Africa, the other from West Africa.

Young adults performed worse than any other age group. Boys aged 15 to 21 failed to spot nearly 50 per cent of the mistakes – which included realy, eght and litterature. Girls the same age missed 33 per cent.

Although 70 per cent of younger people bragged to researchers that they were good at spelling, they made three times more basic mistakes than volunteers aged 41 to 50.

The test, by researchers from Ulster University showed that, overall, older volunteers were better at spelling. Women aged 31 to 40 spotted more than 75 per cent of mistakes and men over 41 more than 80 per cent.

In a second test, volunteers were given three alternative spellings of 24 words – including *address, adress* and *addres* and *definitely, definately* and *defnitly* – and asked to pick the correct one. Again those aged 41 to 50 performed best, correctly identifying more than 90 per cent. The youngest girls identified less than 70 per cent while boys found only 60 per cent.

Although the tests showed women were generally better at spelling than men, there were signs the gender gap is absent among those aged over 41.

Professor Loreto Todd, who carried out the survey for Bloomsbury Publishing, said, 'We used everyday words that schools focused on and in one test simply asked people to pick the correct answers. It is not as if we were asking the youngsters to spell *idiosyncrasy* – we all ought to be able to get *receive* right.'

Yesterday, the survey was seen as further evidence of the devastating legacy of poor teaching in British schools during the 1970s and 1980s, when progressive theories were at their height in primary schools and mixed-ability teaching was common in a new breed of comprehensive.

The researchers say four to 15 per cent of today's school-leavers are functionally illiterate. In 1912, the illiteracy rate stood at just two per cent.

The editor of a new Bloomsbury dictionary which lists misspelt words as well as the correct versions said the findings show spelling is in crisis.

Dr Kathy Mooney said, 'You see a stepping-up of spelling ability with age. This could be because people were educated differently, or because spelling skills improve over time anyway though there are probably elements of both. The older age group had a different educational experience in their youth and that may help them spell better.'

The reasons for the difference in spelling ability are complicated, but it does not get away from the fact that younger people should and could do better.

✳ ✳ ✳ **BREAK ...**

Waffling Matilda – Jeremy Lawrence

The accompanying poem was the winning entry in a *Spectator* competition for a verse cautionary tale a la Belloc for a modern child. The author is a QES member and lives in South Africa. Our congratulations!

Matilda, aged fifteen, was Prone
To use her Mobile Telephone
(A present from her doting Dad)
From dawn till dusk; the creature had
No Self-Restraint. I'm on the Train,
I'm at my Desk, I'm Home again . . .
Thus would the dreary girl relate
Each Instant of her tedious Fate.
And then one day a horrid Ache
Assailed her inner Ear. 'Please take
Yourself to bed!' the Doctor cried.
Soon after that Matilda died.
And at the Autopsy they learned
Her radiated brain had turned
Into a sort of Nuclear Stew -
Her Phone Bill was Horrific too.

PARDON MY PROPER ENGLISH

Raymond Coleman

Modern scientific terminology needs reappraisal. The English language, with its rich vocabulary and means of expression, has emerged as the lingua franca of scientific communication, prompting the thought that perhaps the term should be replaced with lingua anglica. Yet, that wouldn't be quite accurate, because many scientists claim that the true language of scientific meetings and manuscripts is broken English.

Latin, which provides considerable insight into scientific terminology, was a compulsory requirement for university studies in science or medicine when I was educated in England half a century ago. Today, knowledge of classical languages by scientists is extremely rare. Incorrect use of the language and poor writing skills are very common, even by scientific manuscript authors whose native tongue is English.

The US dominance in science has resulted in scientific journals adopting mid-Atlantic spelling and idioms, with the unfortunate erosion of classical English spelling and grammar. Split infinitives – to greatly disagree, for example – are permitted. Mid-Atlantic spelling has resulted in the death of the diphthong: estrogen, fetus, anesthesia, pediatrics, and the like, have become the norm (a hideous word), which is not surprising for a country where sox replaced socks, jail usurped penitentiary or correctional institution, and butt replaced buttocks.

Even more galling has been the add-the-suffix, lose-the-letter phenomenon: signalling reduced to signaling, cancelling shortened to canceling. The widespread adoption of mid-Atlantic spelling (no 'l' lost yet!) is now an accepted fact of life; English scientific journals retaining classical English spelling are now the exception. How many scientific journal publishers even retain a style editor to ensure compliance with grammatical English?

More annoying during the last decade has been the trend to create unsuitable scientific terminology. The molecular biologists are especially guilty of this, with their discoveries of new proteins and functional proteomics. We now encounter transcriptomes, proteasomes, polonies (polymerase colonies), multiplexed arrays, photoaptamers, and electroporation. Proteins are described as combinatorial or compartmentalising. How did we allow such unsuitable descriptive terminology as trafficking to creep into the scientific literature? This conjures up unfortunate connotations of drug-peddling or sex-trading. Admittedly, not all the new descriptive vocabulary is bad. We have moonlighting molecules (which do more than one job) and cascades of molecules.

Introducing new terminology is inevitable, but let us choose acceptable words and expressions while replacing unsuitable euphemisms commonly used in the life sciences. Are laboratory animals really sacrificed (killed) and euthanised (mercy-killed!)? Can we not find more suitable words for paradigm or algorithm? Or express? Or manifest?

A further trend involves the introduction of novel combination words. This, in part, may result from computer programming, where our children accept goto as a single word, and Internet domains consist of multiple, unhyphenated words. The advent of combinatorial neopolysyllablism has led to many clumsily elongated and unpronounceable words, even for native English speakers. Whereas before, we were occasionally surprised to find a word such as pseudohypoparathyroidism, we now have thermochemiluminescence, bioinformaticians, immunophoto-bleaching, and pharmacogenomics.

This tendency to let's-connect-the-syllables has inevitably led to the widespread use of abbreviations, commonly resulting in papers that appear to have more abbreviations than text. These, however, are not always apt. Analytical is commonly shortened to Anal, resulting in Anal Biochem, a term that conjures up proctological connotations and gets categorised as pornographic in Internet searches!

The rise of feminism in the United States and politically correct terminology has also resulted in the introduction of clumsy, gender-neutral vocabulary such as chairperson – we no longer can use the term man to represent the human species. Is it only a question of time before demands are made to reclassify Homo sapiens or – good grief, how inane – to rewrite the Bible and classic literature in PC mode?

What can be done to ensure that suitable language and terminology are used in scientific journals? The sentinels are in place: we still accept the taxonomic system of Linnaeus, and the Anatomical Association of America has international committees to consider and approve terminology in anatomy and embryology. Moreover, the Royal Microscopical Society has spent considerable time defining microscopy terminology. Perhaps we need to establish or re-establish active academic committees to propose and approve new terminology in molecular biology. Adopting editorial standards is both useful and welcome and has been achieved in the past by introducing the *Systéme International d'Unités* in scientific journals in the 1970s and by standardising the format for references and journal title abbreviations. Terminology regulation is important, especially when there is rapid evolution of topics or language. I would like to propose greater debate regarding new scientific terminology which is easily understood, mellifluous, and possibly of classical derivation. This may involve establishment of national academic language boards to debate the merits of new vocabulary and propose new terms to be adopted by scientific literature editors. Each journal should encourage language watchdogs to complain about misuse of words or unapproved introductions. Can we meet the challenge, and preserve some of the elegance of well-written English?

THE CULT OF THE CROSSWORD

Roy Dean

What is the world's favourite intellectual pastime – is it chess, bridge, mah-jongg, backgammon, Scrabble? No, it's none of these – it's solving crossword puzzles.

The crossword puzzle is one of the most universally popular inventions of the twentieth century. In Britain alone, several million people enjoy their daily dose of puzzling. It's estimated that over 80 per cent of the world's daily newspapers carry some form of crossword, as well as many weekly papers and magazines.

The crossword appears to be a combination of the old acrostics and word squares which date back to ancient Greece. The first one was devised in 1913 by Arthur Wynne, an English journalist working on the New York *Sunday World*. Looking to provide his readers with some entertainment, he composed a diamond-shaped grid with all the words interlocking and simple definition clues. He called it a Word-cross.

But it wasn't until April 1924, with the publication by Simon & Schuster of the first crossword puzzle book, that the craze took off. It immediately swept America and dominated social life. It got so bad that dictionaries had to be provided on trains so that commuters could do their puzzles.

A scornful editorial in the London *Times* in December 1924 noted that 'All America has succumbed to the crossword puzzle …' The crossword is a menace because it is making devastating inroads on the working hours of every rank of society. But two months later *The Times* had to admit that the craze had crossed the Atlantic with the speed of a meteorological depression.

The Times itself held out as long as it could, but in the end it bowed to public pressure and published its first crossword on 1 February 1930. It was one of the first daily papers to move away from the simple definition type of clue and introduce the cryptic clue which has to be unravelled before the solver can arrive at the answer. Its diamond jubilee in 1990 was marked with great celebrations and worldwide coverage.

Though not the hardest of its kind, its consistent qualities of sophisticated wordplay and sly humour have won it a reputation as the most famous crossword in the world. It frequently features in novels, plays and films where the author wishes to establish a character of high intelligence. The annual *Times* national crossword championship, which has been held since 1970, attracts up to 20,000 entrants, and the final is a most exciting event as the keenest minds in the country work through four puzzles against the clock.

Why should the cryptic crossword have developed only in Britain? One answer is the Englishman's fondness for wordplay. The 1920s were a period when the country house party was at its height, and it was customary for people to settle down to charades and pencil-and-paper games after dinner. Edward Powys Mathers, a critic, poet and translator, picked up this tradition and translated it into the crossword, calling himself Torquemada after the Grand Inquisitor. Secondly, the English language has evolved over time as a melting pot of words derived from many sources. In addition to the Romance and North European languages which form the basis of the English tongue, there are words brought back by Britons from the former colonies, infusions from Chinese and Russian, contributions from Turkish and Arabic. Greek provides the basis of political thought, science and technology, Latin for religion, medicine and the arts.

English has eagerly taken in everything. Consequently the language contains many words with multiple meanings, deriving from completely different roots. Even short words like 'set' can have a hundred different meanings. And it is not uncommon for a single word like 'round' to serve as noun, verb, adverb, adjective and preposition. These ambiguities are seized upon by crafty crossword compilers who manipulate the language to their own ends to confuse and mislead the solver.

Thirdly, the English language is unique in possessing so many short words which can be used to make up longer ones to which they are in no way related. Take the word 'insignificant' for example. It breaks down neatly into in-sign-if-I-can't. Or 'refrigerator', which becomes ref-rig-era-tor. Tricks of this kind are the meat and drink of crossword compilers. With the most sophisticated practitioners of this form of literary fun, brainwash may be broken down as bra-in-wash and clued as 'bust down reason'.

Anagrams are no longer indicated by the symbol 'anag' in brackets, but by words in the clue suggesting confusion, error, drunkenness, building, possibility and so on. Thus, 'The President saw nothing wrong' may be construed as 'Washington'. Taking this to its highest form, the whole clue becomes a definition of the answer, as in 'Thing called shaky illumination?', giving 'candlelight'.

Then there are many instances of one word slipped inside another to make a third, as in 'ca(bare)t', 'come(lines)s' and 'th(ink)ing'. Sometimes a word is hidden; for example, 'Prime Minister seen in the Atheneum' gives 'Heath'.

Another popular device is words that sound alike: wether, weather and whether are typical of this kind. In some cases a foreign import can sound like an English word: the rubber substance 'gutta-percha' becomes the street urchin 'gutter-percher'.

The crossword compiler has all these tricks up his sleeve, and many more. His tool is the English language in its infinite flexibility, and he uses it to baffle the solver in a devious but entertaining fashion. If you are looking for mental stimulation – and an excellent way of enlarging your vocabulary – why not try an English cryptic crossword?

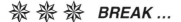 BREAK ...

It's fantastic (or is it?) – Peter Grafton

The verses below may be sung to the tune, Wir Pflügen, of the hymn 'We plough the fields, and scatter the good seed on the land' (Ancient & Modern No. 483 or New English Hymnal No. 262), with or without its not unsuitable repeated chorus.

The English language, which we're taught, is really quite
    elastic.
Its great and wise vocabulary enables us to glean
From its vast storehouse, in a manner almost orgiastic,
Such of its verbal stock as can express just what we mean.

In doing so, we must, of course, avoid the pleonastic
Interspersion of a surplus, which might reason overreach.
Instead, the words employed should be precise and not too
    plastic,
If one's clarity of thought's to be reflected in one's speech.

The subtle shades of meaning, which reside in words
    scholastic,
Are intended to be utilised in most effective ways.
In stating one's opinion, whether modest or bombastic,
One should leave no room for doubt, inducing intellectual
    haze.

So, when describing that o'er which you feel enthusiastic,
Whether excellent, remarkable, enjoyable or splendid,
Incomparable or marvellous, don't just say "It's fantastic".
(Unless, of course, referring to this homily, now ended!)

PRONUNCIATION IN MODERN TIMES

Adrian Willliams

JF Bailey's recent description of the BBC's consultation on pronunciation, the conclusions of which were published in 1935, interested me greatly – and not principally because of the conclusions themselves but because of the eclectic list of words canvassed by the investigating Committee on Spoken English.

Consultation was sought on nine words: *capuchin – poteen – decor – studdingsail – stern – salicylate – longeron – scaramouch – troche.*

This is a curious list. It is not at all clear what purpose the Committee had in mind when it chose this set of words. Is there not a mid-20th-century whiff here of those official enquiries that seemed to say, 'You don't need to know why we ask these questions – just give us the answers when you are asked?'

What words would we choose for today? I offer my own selection – a selection made because I hear the words used frequently (unlike the selection of the Committee on Spoken English). I shall not be shy about saying which pronunciation I prefer, but I will not paint myself into a corner by insisting that my preference is the correct choice. I admit that, when my choice is disdained in the broadcast media, I shout loudly at the radio or television – though my intervention has made no difference so far, alas.

First, there is a whole class of polysyllabic words in which the emphasis has crept backwards in recent years. Let us take, as the standard-bearer of this class, 'lamentable' which, lamentably, is now often pronounced 'la<u>men</u>table'. Other words suffering the same treatment are: 'irrefutable', 'controversy', 'comparable', and 'formidable'. There is a counter-argument sometimes mounted to the effect that, since the Greeks never put the stress further forward than the pre-penultimate syllable, we should do the same; but the argument could only ever be carried when applied to words of Greek origin, and anyway soon fails in the face of undisputed usages such as sensitively.

'Comrade' has suffered an interesting mutation in the last few years. Broadcasters these days like to say 'comrad', as if seeking to emulate the cry of 'Kamerad' that they have picked up from all those WWII films.

'Memorabilia' is definitely foreign from the start. When I learned Latin years ago, the fourth syllable was short; but now the media-pronunciation is tending towards 'memorabeelia'. A more drastic change has been wished on 'memento', which is now generally offered as (for example) 'Did he leave you any momentoes?' But this could be a manifestation of ignorance rather than a trend in pronunciation practice.

Two words that cause me great difficulty are 'bulwarks' and 'ebullient'. The single l in bulwarks seems to demand a short u; and likewise the double ll in ebullient seems to demand a long u. But it is the other way round, according to my *Concise Oxford Dictionary* (Ninth Edition 1995) (*COD*) – and not even disp. (disputed). I console myself with the thought that a weak pronouncer, like a weak speller, becomes strong when he knows his weakness and can remember when to look words up.

'Harass' is another word that I need to check constantly. *COD* offers two versions, with a note attached: …the stress on the second syllable is common but is considered incorrect by some people. (We may infer that … 'common but' means 'frequent but' – whereas 'common and' would have meant 'vulgar and'. Such are the nuances of the English language.) By contrast, the stress on communal seems to be (as people seem to say nowadays) up for grabs.

Lastly, there is a word that I now forbear to use because my pronunciation of it, although not incorrect, is thus regarded. I refer to 'banal'. In my *COD* (Fourth Edition 1951), two possibilities were offered: 'banal' rhyming with 'anal' or with 'flannel'. The etymology was given as deriving from … the use of the lord's mill [which] was compulsory for all tenants (bannal mill) whence the sense common to all. By contrast, the Ninth Edition (1995) offers two possibilities, both of which put the stress on the second syllable; and by far the more preferred in common usage is the limp-wristed drawl of 'banahl', seeming to invite the listener's sophisticated complicity in deriding whatever object, custom or idea is under discussion.

I deeply resent being driven into the long grass with my preferred pronunciation of 'banal' to rhyme with 'anal'. But, at a QES Annual Lunch several years ago, I invited those around me to give their views, and I have to concede that 'banahl' won hands down. So – at least there's no contróversy about that, then.

Are there other favourite candidates for having their pronunciation wrenched back to where it used to be when I was learning the language? Almost certainly. Will my inveighing against modern practices and trends have any effect? Almost certainly not.

✳ ✳ ✳ *BREAK …*

An EastEnders' Hamlet – Michael Holt

HAM is rolling a roll-up, which he eventually lights.

HAM: Do you, or don't you? Top yourself, I mean.
At the end of the day, why go on, eh?
You work your butt off, make a bob or two,
Only for the taxman to steal it back.
Rum do, life. Bit of a lottery, really
Which I do twice a week, never won, tho'.
Then, strike me!, the missus (who's never off
The bloody mobile) scarpers with the lot,
Taking with her my young bit on the side!

Good grief! The scheming bitch then goes to court
And some old fart of a judge, taken in
By her tears, grants her maint'nance! Jesus wept!
My life down the pan, I was tot'lly gut'ed.
So it's back home alone to porn on Sky,
A sixpack, and the old five-knuckle shuffle.
Watch all the daytime soaps, Match of the Day . . .
All that dosh they make, Becks and them with their BMWs!
Nuff to make you puke.

If I'm honest, I wouldn't half mind going
On *Who Wants To Be A Millionaire?*
(Basic'lly, it's all down to the computer,
Ennit? Bit like God, it knows all about us -
Our destiny, our bank balance – all that
Money we have to make case we don't die -
Our hang-ups, who we're living with. Chances are
It even knows when our number's up. Awesome!)
Here's the game plan: bit chancy, Fifty-Fifty.
The bottom line is you mightn't win. 'Kay,
Phone a Friend. Not got one, Chris. Only joking.
Ask the Audience? Nah, do me a favour.
So dim, that lot, they can't find the remote.

I go to a party down the Queen Vic
Not a real party, no one got brahms -
And I get done for illegal possession!
Yeah, straight up. The last ruddy straw. I mean,
What is the bleeding point of going on?
Quit while you're ahead, mate, who'll give a stuff?
A handful of tabs, a little zizz – sorted.

He observes the smoke curling up from his fag.

Can't say I fancy, tho', the thought of when
It's, like, Shuffle Off To Buffalo time,
Going up in smoke at the local crem.
Mug's game, life, if you ask me ... *(Sees OPHIE)*

Omygawd!
It's Ophie. *(To her)* For starters you can naff off
To a refuge.

OPHIE: No, wait …
*She frantically looks at MR POLLY (unseen by HAM). He, a
fan of EastEnders, mimes 'Talk' with his hand.*
Ham, we must talk.
*MR POLLY gives her the thumbs-up sign. He approves of
cliches.*

*[Exegetical note: What would an early Elizabethan have
made of this take on the soliloquy? Shakespeare did two
earlier versions of it before he hit on the one we all know.]*

ANYONE FOR LUNCHEON?

Sir Andrew Leggatt

Samuel Johnson was content to define both 'luncheon' and 'lunch'
neutrally as a kind of meal between breakfast and dinner. Yet the
choice between lunch and luncheon has a long and chequered
history. The OED speculates uncertainly that lunch may have been
derived from lump by analogy with bump and bunch, and that
luncheon may have been derived from lunch by analogy with
punch and puncheon. But whatever their origins, they have been
in competition ever since.

In 1796 James Gillray gave us the revolting spectacle of John Bull
Taking Luncheon: it was enough to put anyone off the meal
altogether and the word itself may have suffered. Byron's Juan
restored some respectability in 1823: *His afternoons he passed in
visits, luncheons, lounging and boxing.* H Best took sides in 1829:
*The word lunch is adopted in that glass of fashion, Almacks, and
luncheon is avoided as unsuitable to the polished society there
exhibited.* In 1855, Mrs Gaskell remarked that, *They did not*

scruple to make a call at each other's houses before Luncheon.
But in 1865 Trollope preferred, *Lunch was on the table at half past one*. In Victorian times neither word was yet predominant.

When for the entertainment of Queen Mary in 1921 the Domestic Bursar of Balliol sent Curzon a specimen menu beginning with soup, the menu came back endorsed with a reproof from Curzon: Gentlemen do not take soup at luncheon! Presumably queens did not do so either. The continuing dispute is epitomised by the account in Webster's *Dictionary of English Usage* of an argument in the 1920s between the American writer William Dean Howells, who liked lunch, and his wife, who preferred luncheon. To settle this dispute, they looked in the *Century Dictionary*, where Mr Howells was pleased to find that he himself was given as authority for preferring lunch. His wife, however, declined to regard him as an authority. This tension still reflected the mood of the wider public.

In 1926 HW Fowler attacked the notion then prevalent that common synonyms such as lunch should be translated into formal words like luncheon. He said in *Modern English Usage* that:

> *they are not the plain English for what is meant, not the form that the mind uses in its private debates to convey to itself what it is talking about, but translations of these into language that is held more suitable for public exhibition. We tell our thoughts to put on their hats and coats before they go out ...*

So it was that in the 1930s Cole Porter informed us that Miss Otis regrets, she's unable to lunch today, and from WC Fields we learned that 'Some weasel took the cork out of my lunch.' In 1942 Evelyn Waugh looked back to an earlier age, when Lady Peabury had been brought up to believe that to read a novel before luncheon was one of the gravest sins a gentlewoman could commit. In more modern vein Noel Coward, when asked, while watching the Coronation, who the man was in the carriage with the redoubtable Queen of Tonga, replied, 'Her lunch.' In the second edition of *Modern English Usage* (1965) Sir Ernest Gowers took the uncompromising line that:

few things contribute more to vigour of style than a practical realisation that the sovereign or dominant or proper or vernacular or current names, are better than formal words.

Thereafter Robert Heinlein reminded us that TANSTAAFL means 'There ain't no such thing as a free lunch'; Jilly Cooper counselled us never to drink black coffee at lunch on the ground that it will keep us awake in the afternoon; and Stephen Sondheim proposed a toast to that invincible bunch – the ladies who lunch – for charity.

Nowadays there are many particular types of lunch: school, working, free, light, packed and ploughman's, while lunch, not luncheon, governs time, breaks, hours and boxes. If we are absent in the middle of the day it is usually to lunch that we are out, although colloquially out to lunch means crazy or insane. But whereas luncheon baskets, like luncheon cars, have receded into the past, and luncheon meat is going that way, even today we have luncheon vouchers, and luncheon clubs abound, catering for interests as diverse as art, tai chi, bowls, chiropody and audiology. Nor should we overlook the availability from English Heritage of packs of Silver Rudolph Luncheon Napkins (not Serviettes), featuring an image of Rudolph the Reindeer with his red nose on a silver red and gold background.

The dichotomy between lunch and luncheon was summed up by Robert Burchfield in the third edition of *Modern English Usage* (1996) when he commented more diplomatically than his predecessors that 'The suitability of one of these rather than the other is a matter of discreet (and often delicate) contextual choice.' Most of us no longer tell our thoughts to put on their hats and coats before they go out, but it has to be admitted that luncheon is still used to refer to a formal midday meal for a group of people, often as part of a meeting. Although we may no longer give luncheons ourselves, there may nevertheless be occasions when we are invited to them. So we should respect the feelings of those who would not think they were getting their money's worth if they were only attending a lunch.

FIGURE IT OUT

Adrian Williams

I was thirteen years old. For most of the term, the class had been slogging away at Parsing (we were hot on Parsing in the 1950s) and, when our English teacher introduced Figures of Speech to break the monotony, I took to the concept like a duck to water …

But enough of the simple **simile** – our teacher briefly touched on **metaphor**, and the awful solecism of the **mixed metaphor**, before he opened the door on an exotic paradise of Figures of Speech, each with its weird Greek name and attendant example.

I recall that next for consideration was **litotes**: an assertion by means of understatement or negation. The example offered in those days continues to be wheeled out today: *I am … a citizen of no mean city* (St Paul, Acts 21.39). Litotes is often to be spotted on our linguistic scene – so much so that it falls into the common or garden category. Prunella Scales as the hotel check-out cashier in a TV advertisement for a credit card: *We're no stranger to the bar, are we, sir?* An associated device is **meiosis**, in which circumstances are intentionally understated: *Don't worry about me, chaps! – it's only a scratch.* And its familiar opposite deserves a mention: **hyperbole**, as in – *He's got a carbuncle on his nose the size of a small potato.*

Zeugma, the yoking of two unassociated words by one word, is less common. It is a somewhat mannered device, as evidenced by the traditional examples of: *He took his hat and his leave* and *She left in a flood of tears and a sedan chair.* Sightings nowadays seem rare to me, although I recently took pleasure from *Our generation stood for order, deference, and the National Anthem in the cinema.* There is debate on the difference between zeugma and **syllepsis**, but the debate seems to be of interest more to students of classical rhetoric than to students of modern linguistic practice, and I will therefore not pursue it, and for the same reason will pass over **prozeugma, mesozeugma, hypozeugma** and **diazeugma**.

But let us not ignore (because this is *Quest*, after all) the deplorable instances of grammatical syllepsis found in such constructions as *We have, are, and will continue to dedicate ourselves to the service of the local community.*

Here thou, great Anna! whom three realms obey / Dost sometimes counsel take – and sometimes tea. Pope's couplet from *The Rape of the Lock* is another example of zeugma (or, arguably, of syllepsis); but I first came upon it as an example of **bathos** – the use of mild ridicule for rhetorical effect. **Hypozeuxis** works in the opposite direction, building up the effect from the beginning. Here, **zeuxis** has the same Greek root as *zeugma*, but the hypo-prefix indicates the opposite of zeugma: phrases that could be yoked are left unyoked, for rhetorical effect. A stirring example comes from Winston Churchill's famous broadcast: *We shall fight on the beaches, we shall fight on the landing grounds, we shall fight in the fields and in the streets, we shall fight in the hills; we shall never surrender.*

An infrequent but popular inhabitant of the linguistic demesne is **oxymoron**: the placing together of two apparently contradictory terms – for example, *He passed his time in successive periods of intense idleness.* My wife recalls, among her former schoolmates, someone who was her best enemy – a coinage that is original without being catty. Sadly, oxymoron is often used in an unkind and disparaging way: *a famous Belgian, an interesting Canadian, military intelligence* – or is that an oxymoron? (Might this usage be termed anoxymoron, perhaps?)

Synecdoche is a device whereby a more inclusive term is used for a less inclusive one or vice versa, as in *Italy won the World Cup* or *There were 40 guns on the moor that day.* When we hear of the White House, the Vatican, the House of Lords and so on, as issuing a statement or taking a decision, we are hearing a **metonymy**, wherein the whole is represented by one of its attributes. In similar vein, *Don't put your daughter on the stage, Mrs Worthington.* Metonymy is sometimes referred to the container for the thing contained – the stimulus of a plaintive attempt by James Thurber to get his English teacher to admit its counterpart, the thing contained for the container, the example he offered being, *He hit her with the milk.*

Thurber argued that the use of milk to stand for milk-bottle made the case for a new Figure of Speech; but perhaps he should have been satisfied with **aposiopesis**, the device whereby an effect is achieved by the simple omission of a word or words, as in: *I haven't the foggiest* or *Do me a favour!* Aposiopesis is one of a family of usages that depend for their effect merely on the ordering or placing of words, or their omission. Other members are **hyperbaton**, in which the familiar order of words is changed (*This, I must see!*), **parataxis**, where phrases are placed side by side without any apparent connexion (*I need a drink, I'm whacked*), and the **transferred epithet** (*The ploughman homeward plods his weary way*).

And to what constructive use can we put this knowledge? None at all, in my view. Figures of speech comprise a range of arcane concepts that are essentially sterile. Knowledge of them leads to nothing. I cannot imagine that Churchill, stumped for a phrase, would say to himself, Time for a spot of hypozeuxis. I cannot imagine that an interview-panel would say of a candidate, 'An effective user of Figures of Speech, don't you think?'

But, for me, they were better than Parsing all those years ago, and I continue to enjoy Figure-spotting in the linguistic landscape, occasionally coming across types (or names, at least) new to me: **asyndeton, anaphora, paraprosdokian** ... Wikipedia lists about 120. Clearly, more research is needed. Er ... **Irony** ...

✳ ✳ ✳ *BREAK ...*

Classroom clangers – TG Cawte

John Muir, a Scottish schoolmaster has collected a number of amusing 'howlers' in his book 'Classroom Clangers' *(Gordon Wright £1.95).*

Here are a few taken from examination answers:

People who work for the government are *senile* servants
Chequers is a *public house* belonging to the Prime Minister.
Transparent is something you see through, for example a key-hole.
A *rudder* is used for milking cows.
In reply to a question on pronunciation, Muir asked 'Where do you put the colon?' 'On the fire, Sir,' said a pupil.
During the war, we needed to increase our supplies, so the Public Parks were turned into *elopements.*
Sir Francis Drake's famous words on Plymouth Hoe were rendered 'the Armada can wait: my *bowels* can't.'

HYPHENS

Adrian Williams

The origin of this article came from my experience of settling down to watch the first programme in a new and much-heralded television series on aspects of cosmology. The opening panel came onto the screen to introduce Part 1 thus:

Looking for earth
like planets

I was confused. I tried reading the words several ways. None of my attempts led to a conclusion that made sense. The words had vanished from the screen, and I had missed about ten seconds of the opening argument, by the time I twigged that the title was 'Looking for earth-like planets'. I was annoyed. As a viewer, I should not have been annoyed, and certainly not that early on.

The writer owes the reader the courtesy of hyphens, to help the process of understanding what is written without the readers stumbling or needing to re-read to grasp the meaning. Standard textbooks give rules for hyphenation: *Correct English* (Phythian, Hodder & Stoughton, 1988) is a good example of a textbook whose rules and examples, if one can learn and remember them, will serve the writer well in most circumstances.

In his section on hyphens, Phythian makes the general comment that 'Anything that causes even momentary doubt in the readers mind should be avoided.' For me, that is the guiding precept that effectively subsumes all others. If a writer follows it, and rereads his work before going into print, there is no need for the memorisation of rules, the chortling over 'extra marital sex' (every grammarians favourite example, to judge from the text-book evidence) or the avoiding of 'two monthly meetings' in favour of 'meetings every two months'. I prefer 're-read' and 're-invent' (although my *Concise Oxford* 1995 prefers 'reread' and 'reinvent'); I put a hyphen into 'fulllength' and 'semiinvalid' on purely aesthetic grounds, as (I am sure) most people would. What about 'cooperation'? Burchfield's Fowler explores 'seaurchin' and preferable options. With words such as 'recover' and 're-cover' there need be no debate, since the two forms have entirely different meanings.

The main cause of confusion with hyphens today comes, I think, from the modern tendency (particularly in writing on technical subjects) to use nouns as adjectives. 'Rough terrain equipment' is a case in point; 'overdue payment record printout' is another. I made heavy weather of this opening to a recent film critique:

In DreamWorks new digimation romp woodland creatures make war on suburbia

(though I concede that a comma after romp is the more useful of the two marks needed to clarify this phrase). I spent time trying to decode an advertisement that began,

We know where you pick up your cash in hand payments ...

(perhaps because my sheltered life has protected me from the temptation to seek or accept cash-in-hand payments). Newspaper headlines are a constant source of confusion: for example, 'Honours row over shooting blunder policeman'. (Shooting being such an alarmingly active participle, its use as a gerund can easily lure the reader down the wrong path, as in 'A part of the moor near the hotel is reserved for shooting guests.')

Usually, writers today do not use hyphens freely enough. There is one undesirable usage, though, which is on the increase: the hyphenating of phrasal verbs in statements such as 'He promised to take-up the challenge and sort-out the problem.' Why is this usage undesirable? Because it misleads the reader into reading the hyphenated noun that is seen in phrases such as 'The take-up was low.' And why is it on the increase? I can only conjecture: perhaps it is an a-little-learning-is-a-dangerous-thing situation.

A writer's weak hyphenation should at least be consistent. A strange failure of consistency appeared in *The Daily Telegraph* recently, when the Consumer Affairs Editor reported on Tesco and its rejection of traffic light-style food labels. In his next paragraph, he referred to front-of-pack nutritional information, so he clearly understands the value and power of the hyphen-strung phrase – but he didn't apply his knowledge consistently. The newspapers are unfailingly consistent in their use of hyphens in human interest stories containing the adjectival phrase, (for example): 'Fit and active father-of-two Garry Penderby'; but I thought that a recently spotted instance of 'grandfather-of-three' was stretching consistency (or perhaps human interest) too far.

In sum: if a hyphen keeps my reading-momentum going, I want it to be provided. If a hyphen is otiose, I want it removed so that it doesn't irk me. In the foregoing comments, I have used hyphens in the hope of honouring Phythian's precept: 'Anything that causes even momentary doubt in the reader's mind should be avoided.' Did my hyphens work for you?

The quotation on pages 12 and 13 is from *My Early Life* by Winston Churchill

ACKNOWLEDGEMENTS AND THANKS

All of the items in this book originally appeared in *Quest*, the Queen's English Society quarterly magazine, and several had been published before that in other places.

The small advisory group, Michael Gorman and Sidney Callis – both long-serving members of the Society – and the Editor had immense pleasure in trawling through back issues of *Quest* to find apposite and entertaining articles for inclusion in this anthology, possibly the first of several.

The QES thanks all contributors for their efforts and gratefully acknowledges that earlier permissions to publish material in the magazine will continue into this present book. The editor admits that just a few changes have been made to some of the published pieces but only when there was a need for clarity or updating.

The Society also thanks Christopher Woodhead of The University of Buckingham Press for his great interest in the project, and Nathan Ariss for his inspired illustrations.

ENDPIECE

Herewith two final comments from our cartoonist, Nathan Ariss. If we had let him loose on the entire range of verbal peculiarities in the book, he would have filled dozens of pages. Thanks, Nathan, for adding visual spice and seasoning to the salmagundi of words – Ed.

HORSEFUL CARRIAGE